BUBBLE PROOF

This publication is designed to provide accurate and authoritative information in regard to the subject matter covered. It is sold with the understanding that the publisher is not engaged in rendering legal, accounting, or other professional service. If legal advice or other expert assistance is required, the services of a competent professional should be sought.

Editorial Director: Jennifer Farthing
Acquisitions Editor: Michael Sprague
Development Editor: Joshua Martino
Production Editor: Dominique Polfliet
Cover Designer: Carly Schnur

Kaplan Publishing books are available at special quantity discounts to use for sales promotions, employee premiums, or educational purposes. Please email our Special Sales Department to order or for more information at kaplanpublishing@kaplan.com, or write to Kaplan Publishing, 888 7th Avenue, 22nd Floor, New York, NY 10106.

BUBBLE PROOF

Real Estate Strategies
That Work In Any Market

Tonja Demoff

To my partners who have shared my dream and vision to help the world create more prosperity and abundance with real estate.

Acknowledgments

I feel the greatest form of acknowledgment goes to you, the reader. I honor your dedication to improving your life, the lives of others and globally changing prosperity consciousness. May you find inspiration within the pages of this book that helps you to create what you desire most.

CONTENTS

Introduction

This book is about how to buy your first house wisely, and then use it as your first step to becoming wealthy in real estate. I realize that this may sound brash, like some pie-in-the-sky scheme that can't possibly work. Believe me, I understand—when I was just starting out, even my closest friends said my ideas were ridiculous!

Until I made my first million dollars, that is. After that, they all wanted to know my secrets.

If you'll just give me a few hours and read my book, you'll know how too. You'll see: This is no retread of a late-night TV infomercial. I am living proof that my methods work. And if you follow the advice and guidance in the chapters that follow, I'm convinced that you can become wealthy in real estate too—while protecting your portfolio in any market.

* * *

Many years ago, I had an epiphany: Most homeowners only viewed their houses as a shelter and a fancy piggy bank. True, they understood the basics of mortgages and equity building. But what so few realized was that their houses were also a potential profit center. They had no idea they were living inside a launch site for achieving wealth. In so doing, they missed out on the opportunity of a lifetime: to become rich and actually realize their dreams of financial freedom.

That's my purpose in writing *Bubble Proof*. As a first-time buyer, I want you to set your goals firmly on owning your part of the American dream. I intend to show you how to get started by purchasing the best house you can, in the most affluent location you can find, for the least amount of money and with the maximum amount of "bubble-proofing" safeguards. Then, I want you to go with me on a journey of discovery, where I introduce you to the many ways that you can leverage your first purchase into a wealth-building real estate portfolio. We will go over the mental outlook you must have to be a successful buyer, seller and investor. You will understand why you must sweep away the indecision in your life and decide to follow a new course. I will show you how to focus on the important things in life and how to fold what you learn here into life-changing action steps.

Soon you'll realize that, what worked when you bought your first property can work again and again, and that you *can* develop a solid array of property holdings. Using the tools you'll discover in my book, you will become a careful, informed and successful real estate investor. You'll work with a results-oriented system based upon discipline, hard work and satisfying returns.

I have made my millions as a real estate investor by following my basic procedures religiously, and understanding that money obeys a set of laws. Additionally, like any other goal in life, you have to think as if you're already successful if you want to become a wealthy real estate investor. We will discuss that as well.

*   *   *

I've been interested in real estate since I was 18 years old. The realty business appealed to my sense of independence and unlimited income. So, I enrolled in numerous real estate programs and tried to attend every real estate seminar that came to the local convention center.

I will never forget the day I finally realized that none of these instructors and seminar trainers were really teaching me how to *do* real estate. They were just taking my money. Things came to a head after I had signed on with a supposed real estate development company in San Antonio, where I was living at the time. My job was to visit homes in pre-foreclosure—that is, their mortgages were in default but formal legal action to evict the owners hadn't yet started. My mission: negotiate a "distress" sale with the owners, and my company would provide the financing to close the deal. I faxed several such deals up to my "coach," along with photos and abstracts of titles to the houses. Then I waited, certain that I had exceeded expectations.

Instead, I got the shock of my young life. My coach didn't feel I had any "deals" worth the company's money! Yet I was convinced that all of the deals I had sent were both doable and would be extremely profitable to the company! To this day, I'm sure the company went behind my back later and closed on all of my deals; I didn't stick around to find out. Anyway, that experience finally did it. I set out on the path to learning real estate my way, and came up with *Bubble Proof.*

I refined my *Bubble Proof* system as I progressed. From very modest, early deals in renovating and renting single-family houses, I moved up to more involved deals with small, multi-unit apartment houses. I prefer four- to six-unit buildings as an intermediate step in building a real estate portfolio because of the vacancy factor. When one unit is vacant, it's not a 100 percent vacancy catastrophe, as it would be in my single-family rentals. Instead, the vacancy rate (and my exposure to loss) was reduced proportionally per unit. These days my newest love is condo conversions—especially properties that are deeded for it. I put these buildings under contract and arrange through my brokerage to sell all the units.

As a Realtor, I've won numerous sales awards. But I didn't become the Number 1 REMAX agent because I sold more properties than anyone else. Rather, I made more money than anyone else. I have become a master at making larger commissions on fewer properties. This, again, is a *Bubble Proof* strategy: My goal isn't the number of deals; it's the profit. I'd rather do fewer transactions and create more profit.

A normal year for me entails more than 200 transactions, mostly of the seven- and eight-figure variety. Will I still handle small houses or commercial buildings? I will—but only when I've tripped over them and I can't say no. Yet if I handle three dozen of these small deals per year, that's an awful lot. And let me add that I never reveal my net worth. Having real wealth means you never gloat.

Away from my businesses, I spend a great deal of time as a motivational speaker, inspiring individuals and organizations to move towards their financial goals. In my travels, I've seen time and time again how, with the right motivation, so-called ordinary people become highly successful real estate investors. Many participants, who are perhaps skeptical, hesitant or uncertain of their own abilities, have a great awakening and see how rewarding and accessible real estate opportunities can be. They become willing to change their lives by taking action.

You will find a big difference between my approach and those of other real estate guides. To be sure, there are no gimmicks in my book and I am not trying to make this seem easier than it is. From other authors you may only hear about the importance of special information and ways to get lower mortgage interest rates. From me, you also will hear how certain ways of thinking actually hold people back. But if we change our way of thinking, see challenges as opportunities and then take action, we can change our lives.

*   *   *

Several years ago, economists began using the term "bubble" to describe the incredible yearly increases in the price of an average home in many U.S. markets. Inevitably, when these increases tapered off and home prices glided back to more normal levels, they said the bubble had "burst."

This book's title, *Bubble Proof*, is my answer to them. I firmly believe that the housing market (as well as commercial real estate) will continue to expand and that young, first-time homebuyers have the most to gain from it. I see nothing on the horizon to change my outlook, either—not today or 10 years from today. As long as the United States experiences steady population growth, there will be constant demand for homes. Growth guarantees an ongoing appreciation in residential property values for years to come. Besides, lenders have made it easier than ever to get a mortgage, through lower down payments, lower credit score qualifications, less documentation and more flexible mortgage terms. And even when "hot" markets cool down, home values historically *still* rise by 3 to 5 percent a year. Not many people associated with stocks or bonds can promise that kind of steady annual return.

*   *   *

In "Motivation," Part One of *Bubble Proof,* we explore why you *must* own real estate, and how you can move from dreaming about doing it, to actually drawing up a game plan for success. I discuss how owning a home changes you as a person—by making you part of a community and giving you a stake in society. Most importantly, owning property provides security for you and your family. There is nothing more reassuring for people, as they get older, than knowing they have enough wealth to live comfortably and worry-free.

We also will look at how to "bubble proof" your all-important first home purchase by examining location, lifestyle factors, career arc, family planning and finding the best bargains in town. And, since I'm a licensed Realtor as well as a real estate broker, I share personal tips on how to discover (and keep) a motivated, enthusiastic Realtor. Believe me, the right choice can help you make a winning offer on a great first house, as well as with additional properties later on.

In Part Two, we look at "The Basics" that come into play when you enter the real estate arena. For example, banks and lenders today have many kinds of mortgages and financial tools that buyers can utilize; I'll review their advantages and disadvantages.

You'll also learn about the concept of "risk" and how your credit history and credit score can be your best friend—or worst enemy—when you apply for a mortgage. If your score isn't so great, I'll provide some suggested remedies that will boost your score— and save you thousands of dollars over the course of your mortgage. I'll provide pointers on how you can decide on the kind of property that best suits your needs, and how to figure out what size mortgage you can afford. We'll take a closer look at how to size up neighborhoods and available properties using my "bubble proof" techniques.

And we'll follow along as two of my real-life clients get pre-qualified for a mortgage, find the perfect Realtor, make offers and ultimately close on the house of their dreams.

But we don't stop there, after buying one property. We forge ahead to prepare you to become an actual real estate investor. In Part Three, "Maximize the Ownership Opportunity," *Bubble Proof* builds on your successful first purchase by laying out strategies for acquiring other properties. These range from condos and vacation homes to two-family homes, fixer-uppers, renovations and multi-unit apartment houses. Each type of property has advantages, and by fully embracing the *Bubble Proof* system of strategic thinking, you'll learn to create and complete one deal after another.

You can profit handsomely by skillfully developing a bubble-proof portfolio of holdings. That's the message in Part Four, "You're a Homeowner! Now What?"

As you change from owning just your house, to taking advantage of investment and rental opportunities, you'll realize there are dozens of possible ways to realize profits. Cleverly negotiating a sale, before you even take control of the property, is often a crucial factor in how much money you'll eventually realize from it. Strategy and tactics will have an increasingly important role to play as you progress from deal to deal.

But I believe there's another aspect that we should consider. My own success has been based upon what I call the "mindset of success." Early on, I realized that the main barrier to achievement isn't "being poor" or "being from the wrong side of the tracks." For most people, the stop sign to wealth is *their not believing* that success is possible! So the final chapter compares the points of view of the millionaire with those of the self-restricted nonachiever. Listed side by side, these diametrically opposed opinions will help you understand why you need to adopt the millionaire's ways of thinking, evaluating, acting and even wanting. Your *Bubble Proof* journey concludes once you become indoctrinated with the mindset of fulfillment, achievement and, yes, wealth.

*   *   *

I consider this book as my gift to you. As with any gift, I hope that the person who receives it will like it and find it useful. Writing these chapters was hard work, but the effort was worthwhile if it helps you start a new, happier and better life.

(As companions to *Bubble Proof,* I also have produced several videos and audio CDs, which describe in greater detail some of the key aspects of my system. I mention these tools in a few spots in this book. You can learn much more about me, my companies and products, and my charitable foundation at my Web site:

tonjademoffcompanies.com.)

PART ONE

MOTIVATION

1

Why You Must Invest in Real Estate — and How to Move from Dreaming to Doing

"Forget mistakes. Forget failures. Forget everything
except what you're going to do now and do it.
Today is your lucky day."

—Will Durant

Nothing empowers Americans more than home ownership. It's the cradle of our society and the culmination of our national purpose. Qualify for a mortgage and you lay claim to your piece of the American Dream. Just as importantly, your first house is the ground floor of a promising future—an investment that will help fund your children's college education, and secure your own retirement. Whether you prefer suburban Cape Cods, city brownstones, stately farmhouses or a countryside villa, everyone's your neighbor when you're a homeowner.

Now imagine a different scenario. Think about your first house not as a final destination or ultimate achievement, but as a starting point. Consider it a steppingstone to a better life today, not three decades from now. The fact is, you can have a prosperous, happy future much sooner than you think; security and wealth don't have to wait until you're in your 60s! But first, you will have to break out of your one-home-per customer mindset and enroll in a new school of thought.

The two major focal points of this book are, first, how to secure a foothold in real estate by purchasing your first house; and then, how you can use real estate investing as a means to obtain freedom, flexibility and a better quality of life. This book is not about investing just for the sake of investing. Instead, you'll learn to think about property ownership in new ways—and how your first purchase can be a springboard to the good life. I firmly believe that real estate investing is every American's greatest guarantee of prosperity and the good life.

That's why you *must* invest in it.

*   *   *

Today, nearly anyone can buy a first house. Mortgages abound for every type of budget, and there are even programs that help low-income workers qualify for home loans. Going ahead with a first-time purchase is certainly much easier today than when your parents tried it. They probably had but one choice: a fixed-rate, 30-year mortgage, with 20 percent down. Today, you can be an owner for nothing down, or with a variable monthly payment, or a flexible rate that's below market if fixed-rate mortgages aren't your cup of tea. (More on mortgages in Part Two.) But in the *Bubble Proof* strategy, your first house is just one of many steps. If you follow the courses of action in this book, they will change your life. My strategies can be adjusted to work in any market. What differentiates *Bubble Proof* from other real estate books is this: Your success does not depend on gaining any special "insider's information"; it depends on your taking action. People who are successful take action, time after time, step after step, and know where they are going.

In order to invest successfully over the long term, you have to accept the fact that you will make mistakes. If you invest correctly— that is, according to the rules and the experience you pick up in each transaction, you will have more successful investments that unsuccessful ones. But the truth is that some just don't work out as well as you hoped. But don't let this deter you or throw cold water on your plans. Losing money in a real estate deal is actually a wonderful way to learn a lot in a hurry! Just don't make one or two bad deals into something more than they are; a setback always has a reason, and it almost always has to do with your fundamentals. There is no real magic involved.

And by all means, don't be afraid to fail! People who are afraid to invest tend to count how much they might lose, and rarely give equal time to consider how much they might gain. I find that most people would love to deal in real estate, but that their greatest fear is losing everything they have. Some believe that once they are over 40 or even 50, they have no chance of regaining their wealth. Just by looking at the expressions on some of my clients' faces, I can tell that they've picked up beliefs along the way that are holding them back and really limiting them.

I understand such concerns. I had them too, when I was just starting out. Such beliefs are normal, but at the same time, they are rarely based on reality. You are never too old to make changes! If you're in doubt, change your outlook. Become more attuned to a risk-versus-reward mindset. Entrepreneurs think about what they might gain instead of lose. They look at their risks from a positive viewpoint, as obstacles that can be overcome. Their overriding goal is to make the doors to financial security open wider with every success. Be sure you do the same.

Taking That First Step

"I have learned more from my mistakes
than from my successes."

—Sir Humphry Davy

I believe that you can change your life in an instant—that a single decision in a split second can change your path forever. The catch in real estate acquisition is in knowing how your decisions will most likely affect your financial future, and indeed, your entire life.

Making the decision to become wealthy is only the beginning. It's a hollow promise unless you set your life's course toward achieving financial independence. To me, decisions are only as good as the actions they initiate. Once you decide to take the steps to change your life through real estate investing, you will change as a person. You will feel excited, energetic and unstoppable. This newfound energy and enthusiasm will assist you in creating an action-oriented plan to achieve your dreams.

As I have said, investing in real estate has very little to do with "how to do it" and a lot to do with "act now." You will learn more by doing than by reading or watching. Even the mistakes that you will make will bring you closer to your goals than if you do nothing at all.

Real estate investing has meant total freedom and enjoyment for me in my life. It has given me the pleasure of traveling, branching into new areas and helping many people break free of their economic bonds. Thanks to real estate investing, I have more time for my family and myself than I would in any corporate position. This is what it can bring you as well. You only have to want it badly enough to be willing to do something about it.

* * *

"Freedom is nothing else but a chance to be better."

—Albert Camus

In my seminars, I sometimes meet people for whom buying a house is too challenging. There is too much jargon and all that math when dealing with loans. The commitment it takes seems to overwhelm them. They are not yet ready to do it. And so, they will often come up with justifications (which are actually excuses) for not jumping aboard. I've found that these are the Five Excuses for Doing Nothing:

1. **I don't have the money.** Unless interest rates on long-term mortgages suddenly go skyward, renters and nonowners will have their shot at owning their own piece of America. With little or no money down, almost anyone with a job can own a home—or renovate, move to a larger house, or buy a vacation home or small apartment building as an investment. In fact, lack of money is often a bigger mental barrier than a real-world hindrance. People like you buy real estate every day with little or no money for a down payment. If they can do it, you can too. There are programs for first-time buyers. You can make use of creative financing and seller financing options. I will show you where to look for these options and how to structure the deal.

2. **My credit rating isn't so good.** Here again, you may be sabotaging yourself with a myth. True, your credit rating and credit score are extremely important. It's never a good idea to pay bills late, skip payments or take on too much debt. But even if your credit record is less than stellar, there are ways to increase your score so that you qualify for a mortgage loan. Very often, the only penalty for mediocre credit is that you pay a higher interest rate than someone with good credit does. Yes, your monthly payments cost more—but at least you can get a mortgage loan approved and buy property. Your initial loan can be refinanced later for terms that are more favorable. (We will look into these methods more thoroughly in Chapter 5. This subject is also discussed on my CD, *Credit Repair Secrets*.)

3. **Nothing's available.** In all my experiences, I have yet to see an area where there are absolutely no attractive, affordable properties listed. In these instances, I advise prospective buyers to rethink their situation. Many buyers want the finest house on the best street—but this is *not* the way to make money in real estate. Instead, they should consider buying a house that may need work, or might not be as well appointed as others—and improve it. Others may be looking in the town with the finest schools. Admirable, but perhaps not doable right now. Wouldn't the area's second-best schools suffice? Perhaps being able to commute to work by car is at the top of the list for would-be buyers. Yet there are also carpools, buses and trains serving many locales. Maybe they could even consider buying a townhouse in the city instead of a two-story in the 'burbs. Then the commuting issue is moot. My point is simply this: There are always real estate options.

4. **A house is too much responsibility.** Since you already have the responsibility of paying rent, there's nothing different about making mortgage payments. But more importantly, I believe that you have a responsibility to yourself to achieve financial security through real estate. It truly is the key to a better life. There are responsibilities with home ownership, certainly— upkeep and maintenance is up to you. Being a considerate neighbor is up to you. Making sure you have adequate insurance is up to you. But the benefits are well worth the effort. You get to write off mortgage interest against income taxes while keeping the appreciation in equity. (If you are a renter, your landlord gets to keep the appreciation in equity in the apartment where you're living.)

5. **I won't buy until I'm married.** Many singles have already purchased a home because they have gotten the message that real estate builds long-term wealth. If you are continuing to rent until you meet that special someone, you're missing your chance to establish an attractive portfolio. Don't try to "time" your life's major events. There's no reason to wait when it comes to real

estate. Should you want to live elsewhere after you find some-one, your house will be easy to sell at a profit or keep as an investment. Why continue to throw away money on rent in the meantime?

If you've been making any of the above Five Excuses for Doing Nothing, the time has come for re-evaluation. Instead of finding reasons not to get involved with real estate, use the following pointers to justify a positive course of action:

Four Benefits of Being a Property Owner

Here are the major advantages to buying real estate:

1. Wealth enhancement. For very little money, you can create significant wealth through property price appreciation and your increasing equity.

2. Social enhancement. Property owners become integral parts of the community, and have a vested interest in maintaining safe, comfortable neighborhoods.

3. Tax benefits. There are more tax benefits and government subsidies in real estate than any other economic activity.

4. Borrowing and buying power. As a property owner, you can borrow against the equity in you property to further your real estate goals.

How Real Estate Pays Off

You build wealth from real estate in at least four ways:

1. Price appreciation. Traditionally, home prices rise an average of 3 to 5 percent annually. The value of your property also rises when you remodel and renovate; when your neighbors renovate; and when your town improves the neighborhood with, say, curbs, sidewalks and street lighting.

2. Amortization. You gradually pay off your mortgage loan and increasingly gain equity in your property.

3. Passive income. You can generate income by renting your properties.

4. Tax shelters. You can protect your wealth with the many tax benefits of ownership, rentals, leases and other arrangements.

Most importantly, when you become a homeowner, you unlock the financial power generated by the one-two combination of appreciation and equity buildup. As your home's value rises, so does your equity stake in it. Depending upon your personal situation and the economy, you can tap into your own home and use it to leverage other real estate investments.

Here again, some homeowners may be intimidated by such an arrangement. After all, they may have lived in their houses for years; their houses are their safety blankets, their shelters from an uncertain and, at times, unfriendly world. They tell themselves they cannot bear to jeopardize their home by leveraging its value in the marketplace. Everywhere, they see the risks of taking action; but ironically, they fail to see the much greater risks of doing nothing at all.

People often wake up only after they see other people prosper. They realize that they might have done just as well, if not better, *if only they had acted.* I believe it is a matter of healthy competition instead of simple envy. We all compare our performances with those of our equals, even when we don't realize that we are doing so. When the couple that rents the apartment across the hall invites you to a housewarming at their new home, it is almost impossible not to look at what they have and think that you might have done just as well. You tell yourself that perhaps you will do something next year. However, next year will be no different—except that you will be a year older, probably no wiser, and no richer—unless you make the decision to purchase a home, and then act on it. When you do this, your life changes.

America's Best Offer

Almost all initial real estate purchases are leveraged investments, meaning that the buyer borrows to pay part of the purchase price. Ideally, from a lender's point of view at least, a buyer makes a 20 percent down payment and borrows the rest with 30-year, fixed-rate or adjustable-rate mortgage.

However, there's been a revolution in residential financing and even though the majority of mortgages are still arranged the traditional way, it is possible to pay as little as 3 or 5 percent down. Sometimes, buyers put no money down at all. However it's packaged, purchasing a home with a mortgage has been, and I believe will always be, the best deal in America. Let's go over a typical mortgage so you can see for yourself why a leveraged investment in real estate is such an amazing bargain.

Two of my clients, Tom and Sue, buy a home for $200,000. The couple makes a 20 percent down payment and carries a $165,500 mortgage at 6 percent—$160,000 principal on the house, plus about $5,500 in closing costs and points which have been rolled into the mortgage. Their monthly principal and interest payment is about $992. After including taxes and insurance, let's say they pay $1,340 a month altogether. In other words, it costs Tom and Sue $16,080 a year to service their mortgage loan, pay their property taxes and keep their insurance up to date.

After a year, Tom and Sue decide to sell the house. They find that the house has appreciated 10 percent in value, and is now worth $220,000. At settlement, Tom and Sue get back their $40,000 down, and also receive the $20,000 in property appreciation. What's more, they have been able to apply all their property taxes and mortgage interest payments to their income taxes. Roughly speaking, that's more than a $12,000 deduction. (Remember, during the early years of a mortgage, the vast majority of each monthly payment is applied to the interest portion of the loan, not the principal amount.)

There are capital gains taxes and other incidentals involved in the transaction too. But before these expenses, Tom and Sue have netted $3,920 on an investment of $40,000, after subtracting one year's debt service. This works out to an estimated 9.8 percent return on their money in one year, using very reasonable assumptions. When they compared that figure to the 5 and 6 percent returns they got on their stocks and money market account, they were quite pleased. And at tax time, they had a hefty deduction to offset income taxes and lessen their exposure to the capital gains tax.

Even if Tom and Sue did not sell and their house's value rises by just 5 percent in a year, they still have found themselves a good deal. The house is always there as an investment. They have tax savings and, in the meantime, they can enjoy living in their own home.

I cite the happy story of Tom and Sue, who saw their opportunity and seized it, in order to show what happens to other couples who hesitate and let their insecurities get the better of them.

Several years ago, a friend's daughter and her new husband were renting an apartment in Boston while they searched for their first house. Although they saw many nice, affordable homes, they just couldn't make up their minds. So, thinking it would be wise not to rush into buying, they held off.

As the months passed, however, they began noticing that housing prices were increasing considerably. A year after they ended their search, prices in some neighborhoods they liked had moved beyond their reach. They decided to wait until things "cooled off"; and just two years later, they found they could no longer afford to buy a home in Boston. And when their lease came up for renewal, their rent was nearly doubled, to boot!

If this couple had bought a house when they first started looking, they would now be taking advantage of the equity appreciation in their home. Even if they had invested in the worst house in the worst neighborhood, they probably would have made money. The lesson here is that by doing nothing, they lost out.

As a buyer, you can't realistically expect boom conditions to hurtle your home value upward after you make your purchase. But even in quiet, stable market conditions, if you can make the payments on your mortgage loan, you will have a property that increases in value at a predictable 3 to 5 percent a year. You will not make a short-term financial killing, if that is what you are looking for. However, while you wait for your wealth to grow, you have an affordable house in which to enjoy your life and provide for your financial future. You will come out way ahead in the long run.

What happened to the Boston couple? Sadly, they finally had to leave the city they loved for a distant, albeit affordable, village. Even sadder is this: The opportunity they let slip away is gone forever. That's why I preach that you must buy real estate. For you, the time has come. Don't wait until you too are priced out. Act while you can and that means now!

Seeing Over the Horizon: What Lies Ahead?

Understanding how the real estate market got to where it is today answers a lot of questions about its future. Before the 1990s, there was no real estate market as we know it today. People back then became homeowners, usually with a vanilla, 30-year mortgage, and held onto those homes until some circumstance in their lives dictated that they sell. It simply never occurred to the vast majority of people back then to regard their homes as a way of leverage into other financial opportunities.

The first stirrings of the "new" real estate market we have now consisted of a drop in interest rates for mortgage loans in the early 1990s. In 1990, the 30-year mortgage interest rate was 10.13 percent. In 1993, it was 7.33 percent. Once people took action by refinancing their mortgages for lower rates, they found that they had broken out of their long sleep and were ready to do more.

Agents, mortgage lending companies and other real estate professionals responded by streamlining their procedures. Applying for a loan, getting approval and paying closing costs had been complicated and time consuming up to this point. These stages became simplified, computerized and less costly. What had once taken weeks could now be accomplished in hours, sometimes even in minutes.

Coupled with that was the arrival of widespread Internet listings by brokers, banks, mortgage companies and even government agencies. This explosive spread of information turned the marketplace into a truly nationwide enterprise that never closes or takes a day off. People can view properties from the comfort of their own homes, 24 hours a day, seven days a week. Those who feel intimidated or pressured by agents can conduct self-guided tours. Internet listings reveal what is available, where it is located, and at what price. And some will even provide comparable prices on similar nearby houses (known as "comps") to measure a listing's worth.

That said, there are some things the marketplace still lacks and needs to develop, transparency and fairness being foremost among them. Despite the revolution in mortgage products and more lenient down payment requirements, I still find isolated cases where contract language is baffling, some products have hidden "gotcha" clauses and some buyers really don't understand what, exactly, they've just signed up for. Success is only assured when the market gives people what they want at competitive prices, and everyone is treated with fairness and respect. To me, these must be the underlying forces for the real estate market's continued growth and expansion, and its top priority must be satisfied participants. That is why I have little time for theories or comparisons. As long as the real estate market treats people honestly, large numbers will come to deal, regardless of economic ups and downs.

My Market Predictions

Here are the main reasons why I believe that the real estate market will continue to do very well for at least the next ten years, and why you can feel confident in your life-changing decision to become a real estate owner/investor:

A healthy residential housing market is vital to America's economy. The Federal Reserve will keep inflation tightly controlled to prevent interest rates from spiraling. This will ensure that mortgage money and construction loans continue to flow.

Home prices will continue to rise at their traditional pace, because of moderate supply and increasing demand.

The United States population is expected to increase by 5 percent over the next decade, an addition of about fifteen million people to the population.

Considerable new demand for housing will be created by immigrants, upwardly mobile women and minorities, "empty nest" baby boomers and so-called "Generation Y" young adults.

Senior citizens are living longer and thus becoming more numerous, increasing the demand for vacation homes.

Lenders will continue to trim costs and cut red tape, removing much of the intimidation and delay in buying real estate.

Mortgages will continue to come in ever-increasing varieties, so more people will qualify for a loan.

Popular, buyer-friendly programs sponsored by both the government and private interests will continue to create many new (mostly first-time) homebuyers.

In this new century, Americans have discovered the real estate market as a viable alternative to the stock market. Things have changed, at least for the foreseeable future, if not forever. In the next chapter, I'll show you why real estate is "bubble proof" no matter what the economic forecasts say—and how you can custom-build your first home purchase on *your* terms.

2

Real Estate Is Bubble Proof

"Buy land. They're not making it anymore."

—Mark Twain

Earlier, I touched upon the reasons why real estate is the perfect investment choice. In my opinion, it's as safe as any long-term U.S. Treasury note because it has a proven track record of solid growth. Time and again, real estate has shown that it weathers economic downturns much better than stocks, while in good times having the capacity to rise higher and faster than the equities markets. Done right—that is, with patience, informed judgment and an entrepreneur's savvy—real estate buying and investing should leave you very well off indeed.

Am I saying that *all* real estate is bubble proof *all* the time? No! This isn't a perfect world. Real estate sometimes softens and spooks buyers, lenders and builders. And, frankly, some people will never be convinced that real estate can be a winning investment strategy. They'll point to anomalies, like the post-Katrina Gulf Coast, or the unfortunate collapse of Detroit's auto-based economy or even the latest land-speculation scandal in a retirement community, as their rationale for doing nothing and getting nowhere.

Yes, Katrina was a nightmare that will take years to overcome. One-industry cities are precarious in today's global economy. And unscrupulous land speculators get their kicks by causing a run-up of prices in resorts and retirement areas, then heading out on the midnight train.

But these examples, while sobering reminders of what can go wrong, are exceptions that shouldn't deter you from your goals of buying your first house, then using it as a springboard to buying other investment-grade properties. You can protect yourself, avoid mistakes, and make wise choices if you follow the "bubble proof" methodology.

*   *   *

I have titled my book *Bubble Proof* to explain two things: Call them the "macro" and "micro" concepts of "bubble proofing."

First, the macro: Real estate is bubble proof over the long term because it has always shown itself to be resilient and rewarding. Real estate is always in demand. Someone is always buying, selling or investing in property, so there's always a market for it. Its major segments—residential, rental, commercial—don't move in lockstep, so that a diversified "real estate portfolio" can be built and adjusted for performance.

Even in downturns, some segments of the real estate business actually gain. In the recession of 1999-2001, residential housing was a bright spot in an otherwise sluggish economy. Rates for a 30-year, fixed-interest mortgage were around 5 percent, their lowest levels in at least 40 years. This fueled record housing construction and purchasing that helped keep the recession brief. It also set the stage for the boom years that followed.

I would also point out that, unlike the stock market, real estate trends are foreseeable from a distance. Prior to any up or down movement in the business as a whole, we have reliable predictors: interest rates, home sales figures, building permits and the like, issued monthly and debated endlessly by economists, business reporters and experts.

What's more, real estate investors have the advantage of early warning systems to help us sidestep potential traps. As an example, when too many condominiums are being built in my city, invariably there are economic reports and news coverage forecasting a glut well in advance of its arrival. I can take action accordingly.

Contrast that with a normal *week* on the stock exchange. Some days, market losses can amount to 2 or 3 percent due to some upsetting event: an overseas terrorist attack, an OPEC announcement or a poor blue-chip earnings report. Unless your last name is Buffett or Kerkorian, normal investors can't divine the stock market's next move. But I can tell you where my real estate holdings are headed— and that kind of predictability helps make them, and me, "bubble proof."

That said, I caution against being dismissive of day-to-day economic news. You have to know what's happening in the larger arena in order to comprehend events at the local level. I just don't think it's wise to lurch from one mental place to another based upon anything headlined "newest" or "latest." In our media-saturated nation, having too much information can be just as crippling as having too little; either way, you're still in the dark.

I also want to give you some insights into so-called "bubbles" in the real estate market, because the term itself is bandied about too often with no real context. I trace the word's current meaning to the Japanese economic crisis of the 1990s, triggered by a national real estate and currency collapse; and our own NASDAQ stock market crash of 2000. In both those cases, there was an irrational run-up of valuation, then a frightening disintegration of wealth as each house of cards came tumbling down. The Japanese economy was prone for a full decade afterward. And NASDAQ lost an estimated 70 percent of its value within 30 months of its March 2000 peak.

Compare that with real estate. First, there has never been a national home-price bust. Granted, some local markets take off on a dizzying spin up, only to have a hair-raising descent, as was the case in the first years of the 21st century in places like California, Las Vegas and New York City. But this is neither as commonplace nor as

widespread as some critics claim. In fact, prior to the upturn I just
cited, the last such documented cycle happened in 1994 when median home prices in Honolulu bottomed at 16 percent, according to
Money magazine. Before that? Los Angeles in 1990, where homes fell
about 20 percent due primarily to a troubled aerospace industry. (By
the way, both markets rebounded beautifully.)

Has there ever been a coast-to-coast housing bubble? No, and
there never will be one. Our nation is simply too large, complex and
multifaceted. I think local markets become overheated sometimes,
due to speculation, easy-to-get mortgages and old-fashioned avarice.
Inevitably, prices that zoom upward are going to drop quickly too.
And people watching these markets toss around the word "bubble"
almost out of habit. But that doesn't automatically mean there is a
bubble affecting the rest of us!

*   *   *

Now, for the "micro" explanation of "bubble proof."

This book advocates the purchase of houses, duplexes, condos,
apartment buildings or even office or storefront space *only if* they
meet certain requirements, and therefore are "bubble proof." In
other words, by applying the methods I outline, homebuyers and
investors can bubble proof their investments.

What constitutes "bubble proof" real estate? Obviously, not all
real estate qualifies. I certainly wouldn't advise a client to buy land
on a decaying waterfront, or in a bad neighborhood, where only a
Herculean government program could possibly turn its fortunes
around. But I do recommend that prospective buyers seek out the
countless quality opportunities to acquire and profit from real estate
using the bubble-proof approach. These profit makers spring up
each week and are waiting for you, as a judicious real estate shopper,
to realize their potential.

In the chapters that follow, I'll introduce you to the components that go into bubble-proof purchasing, starting with your first home and then branching into investment properties. For now, though, let's touch on the basics that every deal needs:

- Affordability. Without doubt, this is the most important factor to consider, whether it's your first home or your twenty-fifth condo. This may sound obvious at first, but it's amazing how many people stretch too far and get trapped when their low-interest adjustable mortgage shoots skyward.

- Favorable conditions. It doesn't matter what's happening elsewhere; focus on where you want to buy. Look for markets that are appreciating, and where homes are selling and not sitting. Be sure the nearby area is prospering, not struggling. (Here's how to tell: Find the towns with the best schools, and then go house hunting.) You may have to research newspaper archives, business journals and the Internet for some of this information, but it will keep you from committing a major blunder later on.

- Location. Here's where Realtors earn their stripes. They know the local market, inside out—and about opportunities that you would never unearth on your own. Remember: Your goal is equity growth, not looks, so forget about buying the nicest house on the block. Instead, buy a house that needs work, in the best neighborhood you can find.

- Realism. Buy for today and trust that the future will take care of itself. No market is immune to bumps and dips in the road; but smart buying can overcome nearly every obstacle. Real estate using the *Bubble Proof* tools will not make you rich overnight, but it will over time.

- Common sense. Make sure that any real estate deal you strike makes sense today. If the property is affordable, in a good market, fundamentally sound and has real potential to appreciate, then—and only then—you should pounce. Buying in an area that's only projected to boom is a fool's errand. Let the speculators lose everything instead.

- By meeting each of these requirements, a home or property acquisition meets my criteria for being "bubble proof." It's easy to see how these basic standards mesh into a bulletproof vest, if you will, that protects my investment before I've even placed my down payment. With these safeguards in place, buying your first house should be almost anticlimactic, because you've eliminated the negative factors that can result in disaster.

*   *   *

"Clear your mind of 'Can't.'"

—Samuel Johnson

There is a spiritual element to bubble proofing your real estate endeavors. You must be prepared, mentally and emotionally, in order to be a completely successful homeowner and investor.

In my profession, I help people to do just that. I've benefited from my years of training U.S. Air Force personnel, which hew nicely with my career as a motivational speaker and real estate consultant. I've counseled raw recruits as well as longtime company CEOs. Their personal challenges are varied and often not what you might expect. However, in general, their problems tend to have less to do with the workplace and more to do with their personalities.

Take the Air Force as an example. It has a competitive entry system, and its recruits are bright and above average. However, they are young and their personalities are often not fully formed. This is when training takes hold.

The Air Force knows exactly what it needs from them. It does not need an opera singer or bull rider, regardless of their talents. It needs a pilot, mechanic, weather expert or marksman. To get what it wants, the Air Force teaches them how to maximize strengths and minimize weaknesses. The recruits may not agree with how the Air Force goes about it, but their opinions aren't relevant. They simply have to shape up and deliver what's needed.

In camp, the drill sergeant makes the decisions. The drill sergeant doesn't want to hear about anybody's mom and dad, high school sweetheart or taste in music. Recruits are only expected to make whatever changes are needed to become lean, smart, fully capable members of the best fighting force in the world. Whatever changes are required along the way must be addressed. Corrections must be made. Knowing what needs changing isn't good enough; the recruits must do something about it.

For most recruits, the weaknesses that are easiest to identify— what psychologists term "negative behavior patterns"—are a good place to start. The drill sergeant wants his men and women to identify their behavior patterns and do something about the negative ones.

But in real life, sometimes you must be your own drill sergeant. You need to make your own decisions. From time to time, you need to shout at yourself, "Move it!"

Here's why I'm discussing the importance of personal attitude and motivation before we get into the details of buying property. If you enter into anything with a negative attitude, the results are likely to be less than optimal...less than they might have been.

On the other hand, if you try to overcompensate by becoming unrealistically optimistic, you're going to be disappointed and lose your motivation. The ideal place to be is in between; that is to say, a realist. And to do that, you must take an inventory of yourself. By better understanding your makeup, you can strengthen positive personality traits and diminish negative ones. Find out your character weaknesses and work on them. Knowing your weaknesses enables you to repair them, like cracks in a foundation.

Another point I make in my motivational classes is that individuals are actually two people. To explain: You are the person you know yourself to be, and you are the person whom others see. Bubble proofing yourself calls for you to embark on a quest for personal growth. You will realize that you have work to do in building your character for the challenges ahead. The good news is that you are not stuck with who you are right now. You can change.

Here are some building blocks of character that I've found to be indispensable:

- **Courage.** Have the courage to examine your life, change what you can, and embrace every challenge as an opportunity to learn and grow.

- **Integrity.** Character is developed from the inside out. Tell the truth about the big things as well as the little things. Be honest with yourself and others. Take responsibility and let others know they can count on you.

- **Passion.** This is what makes the impossible, possible. Passion is the driving force within you. You must bring passion into what you do and be passionate about who you are.

- **Focus.** Oprah Winfrey once said about her talk show competitor, Phil Donohue: "It takes too much energy to turn around and see what the other guy is doing." Don't worry about rivals. When you are focused, you are enthusiastic. You feel energy within you, surging and renewing itself.

- **Listening skills.** Steven Covey, author of *7 Habits of Highly Successful People*, put it well when he said, "Seek first to understand, and only then to be understood."

- **Gratitude.** Be thankful for what you have. If you're not thankful now, why do you think you'll be grateful later on?

- **Positive attitude.** Most people are not out to hurt or offend you. Look for the good in people and you'll find it. Our differences are often fewer than our similarities. And the experiences of others are often our best teachers.

The Meaning of Success

"Nothing can stop the man with the right mental attitude from achieving his goal; nothing on earth can help the man with the wrong mental attitude."

—Thomas Jefferson

Success in real estate lies not in the art of the deal, so to speak, but in your own mental attitude toward success.

Success means different things to different people. It is extremely subjective. No two "success stories" are the same. For some, success is paying off their mortgage early and socking away their savings for a second home. Others think it's living in one-half of a duplex and having a tenant pay the mortgage by renting the other half. For others, it's quitting their 9-to-5 job and becoming a landlord and investor. But whatever the definition, success usually requires the same thing from everybody—that you bring your inner life into accord with your outer life.

For example, a typical group of people, gathered at one of my real estate seminars, might seem to have one wish in common: to be successful at real estate. All may be successes, but some will be far more successful than others will. Perhaps luck and IQ will play a part for some, but for others, success will be due mostly to their mental attitude. Their minds are open to achieving. Therefore, when opportunities are presented, they recognize them as such and act on them immediately.

Don't we all do this? Well, unfortunately, we don't. Our minds are stuffed with beliefs that can get in our way when we want to advance. This clutter might include beliefs such as:

- Working *hard* for your money and resisting the concept of working *smart* instead. The truth is that no one thrives on long hours, stress and poor diet. Working smart combines information, confidence and control to tamp down stress and overcome challenges.

- Sticking with old friends through thick and thin. Take along only those who share your evolving goals. They are your true friends. Leave behind those who want to hold you back or who don't care about your newfound interests.

- Believing the myth that your private and business lives are separate. In fact, the way you handle your private life dictates how you conduct your business, and vice versa. *Bubble Proof* success is total—it permeates our lives and can't exist in one part and not another.

- Thinking you must stay in your comfort zone. On the contrary, you will have to leave it in order to buy real estate successfully. To me, "zones" represent the easy way, the route with the least challenge and something that requires the least commitment.

Each of these steps is a commitment to your new life in real estate. They will guide you as you seek out opportunities to excel and move on. Think of them as part of a growth process—a discipline that, each time it is utilized, moves you one step closer to where you want to go.

3

Types of Properties Worth Investing In

Tony and Maureen Wheeler's hugely successful series of *Lonely Planet* travel books started in the 1970s as a single handwritten guide to seeing Asia on the cheap. The couple wrote the booklet to raise cash after going broke on their journey. Today, their company has three worldwide offices with more than 400 employees and another 150 full-time travel writers.

So many businesses start in the same casual way! The participants have only a vague notion of what they are getting into. But they take that crucial first action, only to find one new opportunity after another, which they never would have gotten if they'd done nothing.

In an early *Lonely Planet* book, Tony Wheeler advised readers not to worry so much about itineraries or where to stay. "Just go!" he advised.

So—where do you want to start on your real estate journey? The following five destinations are excellent options and make the most sense:

- First home
- Trade-up home

- Vacation home
- Rental property
- Rehabbing to keep or to sell

Each of these five options has its pros and cons. You need to consider the potential of each, but don't assume that your choice is limited to one. In fact, you can choose all of them, as well as others that we'll touch upon later on. For now, though, let's look briefly at each of the five options I've listed. We'll examine them in detail in later chapters.

Your First Home

"The thing always happens that you really believe in;
and the belief in a thing makes it happen."
—Frank Lloyd Wright

Buying your first home is different from any other real estate investment you will ever make. First, it is a three-part commitment: to yourself; to your partner if you have one; and to the community you enter. You become a person of standing on your street and someone for your local elected officials to reckon with. Owning your own home changes your life. You may have endured politely as other people talked on and on about the home they just bought. (Just as you did as they droned on about their vacation.) It's much more fun when you can turn the tables and have other people listen as you talk about the terrific house you just bought.

Look at your situation. If you don't own a home, then you presumably pay rent. And it's true that, as a renter, you don't have to worry about paying real estate taxes, repairing the furnace or mowing the lawn. When things don't work, you call the landlord. Renting is just so convenient. Is that so bad?

YES! Suppose you pay $1,000 a month in rent. That's $12,000 a year that has gone to the landlord, so that he or she can pay the note on the building where you live, grow equity in the place and enjoy some generous tax benefits as well. What do you get out of the deal? Not a dime. That same money—your money—could be and should be working for you instead of someone else.

Paying rent long term is throwing money away. The longer you do it, the more money you lose. Now, think again about the "convenience of renting" as opposed to owning and building wealth. I hope you can see the folly of being a renter instead of an owner. And to get on the right path, you must step up and buy that first house.

Buying your first home is not the end of the road; it is just the beginning. You don't have the luxury of padding around your apartment in your slippers, looking through the "Homes for Sale" section of the newspaper to find that first house. Remember, this is the first deal of a succession of them—one that you'll use as a template for those that follow. It's time to get busy.

You see, some people wait for months, then years, hoping to buy their first home from a relative or friend, or hoping to hear about an available house in their neighborhood. That's too long. You can't wait for this to happen to you. It's decision time.

Start by asking yourself what kind of house you want and which neighborhoods you like best. If you are picking your hometown because it is the only one you know, you should explore a larger area. When you look in other places, you will be surprised by the variety of neighborhoods and that many of them would make excellent investment choices.

Once you get your basic needs straight in your own mind, you'll save a lot of time and effort by going to a real estate agent. (In the next chapter, I'll discuss how to find an agent that's perfect for you.) Communicate your circumstances clearly to a real estate agent. For example, the agent will want to know what you want, and how much house you can afford to buy. The HUD Home Buying Wish List, also in Chapter 4, will give you some ideas about finding true value in a house.

A good agent will assist you in making these decisions. Don't be too proud to be straightforward with your agent. Like clergy, they hear confessions all the time that are far worse than yours are!

We'll review the other steps in acquiring a house in the remaining chapters of this book.

Trade-Up Home

You may need a bigger home because your family is expanding or because you feel too restricted in the place you currently have. You may have aimed too low the first time you bought and now you need more room and/or amenities. You may feel you have done so well at the low-stakes table that you are ready to play for more. You may be doing it for your partner.

There are a thousand good reasons why people need a better house than the one they have. One reason I would add is that it can be a very smart business move. If you trade up from, say, a $200,000 home to one worth $400,000 without overstretching your financial situation, then you can turbocharge your net worth as your new home's value increases.

You can use the equity you have gained in your present home, and any appreciation in its value, as leverage to purchase a more expensive home. I suggest looking at your next real investment as soon as you became settled in your first home, because this bigger investment will require time to put together properly. You will probably have to wait for your mortgage payments to gain you some equity, or for your present house to gain significantly in value, before you can act. Don't look on this as a frustrating delay, but as a time in which to investigate, make contacts and learn.

Many people wonder whether they should trade up or renovate. You get to keep your present home if you renovate. On the other hand, you may have to live with ongoing construction for much longer than you initially anticipated. One way to decide is to compare your house value with others in your neighborhood. If your home's estimated value is at the top already, you probably should not renovate. You could spend a lot of money on improvements, only to find that your house won't appreciate enough for you to recover the expense and realize a profit when you sell.

Still, finding the right trade-up house is often a big problem too. You've probably grown more particular than you were when you bought your first home. On the other hand, you are probably more confident now than you were then, and therefore more willing to act instantly when you see what you want.

Once you buy, you need to quickly sell the house you are in. Timing your move from one house to the other can be tricky. For more on this and other trading up tips, including the financial aspects, see Chapter 7.

Vacation Home

Your second home could be a weekend retreat, a vacation home, or quite literally a second home in which you spend almost as much time as your first home. All kinds of second homes can be valuable, but vacation homes have traditionally been the hottest properties by far.

About 80 percent of second home sales are of vacation homes. Many are in established resort cities, such as Sarasota and Naples, Florida; Santa Barbara, California; Park City, Utah; and Myrtle Beach, South Carolina. Homes in these areas rose an average of 27 percent in value between 1999 and 2001, according to a National Association of Realtors' survey:

Median second home price

1999	2001	2004
$127,800	$162,000	$200,000–$210,000

A different, smaller survey of 10 select markets found that vacation homes appreciated in price by 22 percent in a 12-month period from mid-2003 to mid-2004. This second survey was conducted by EscapeHomes.com.

The median age of first-home buyers is 32. The median age of second-home buyers is 47. Don't wait until you are 47! Think how much better off you'd be if you were buying your first home at 22 and your second home at 32.

Many buyers of vacation homes are retired people with time on their hands. The growing number of retired Americans, as a percentage of the population, is causing the market for vacation homes to surge even higher than the residential market in general. Another force driving the vacation home market is the 1997 capital gains tax exemption of $250,000 for individuals and $500,000 for married couples. This beneficial change allows people with grown families to trade down in home size and buy a vacation house with the profit.

What's more, Internet listings entice people to check out resort properties in places where they might not have looked otherwise. All in all, the second-home market is driven by several very different forces. In Chapter 9, we'll look at single-family vacation homes and condos, useful things to know about this market, and why I don't recommend time-shares.

Rental Property

The rental property equation is so simple that it is hardly believable. On one side of the equation, you put down a relatively small amount of money on the property purchase price. On the other side, tenant rental payments cover most, if not all, of your mortgage payments, property taxes and maintenance costs. In time, you get to own the building for the cost of your down payment. If this sounds too good to be true, consider this—if you are paying rent now instead of owning, you are already part of this equation—only on the wrong side! There is probably no reason, beyond your unwillingness to act, for you not to be on the winning side.

Rental properties come in all shapes and sizes. Sometimes, you can even divide your own home. Vacation homes in desirable locations often serve as rental properties for much of the year. The first home you own may be a two- or three-family dwelling, perhaps in a neighborhood you could not otherwise afford.

State and local codes vary for multiple dwellings, so you need to consult a knowledgeable real estate agent or lawyer to make sure you conform to them. For example, in some places, fire codes and other regulations affect multi- but not single-unit dwellings. When a rental property consists of more than, say, three or four units, more stringent regulations may apply at state and local levels. Don't be discouraged by this red tape. Many regulations deal with safety, which ultimately protects you as well as your tenants. I suggest to individuals or couples buying rental properties for the first time, that they limit themselves to a maximum of four units per property.

What about collecting the rent? Contrary to expectation, this is usually not a problem. Most tenants simply mail their monthly checks to the address provided. Most of the work involved in a rental property is likely to be in two areas: prospective tenant screening and maintenance.

Having good tenants and keeping the building in good shape are the essential things for a prosperous rental property. One troublesome tenant or a recurring building problem can make life miserable for owner and tenants alike. Time spent screening your prospective tenants is worth every minute you devote to it. Also, the services of a reliable and skilled handyman are indispensable.

Whether you live in the building yourself is likely to make a difference. The further you live from the building, the harder it will be for you to manage it yourself. Retaining a property-managing firm to take care of everything can cost 5 to 10 percent of rental income.

For single rental units, you have the choice of a house or condominium. There is a trade-off involved. A house is likely to require more ongoing personal attention than a condo. On the other hand, with a condo you must pay a monthly, nondeductible maintenance fee—but you don't have to do repairs and upkeep chores. Renting a condo will most likely cost you more than a house would, but your time spent keeping it up is greatly reduced.

The conveniences of condos, particularly for people who live most of the time at a distant location, make them an alluring investment opportunity. In Chapter 10, we will look further into how apartments and condominiums stack up, side by side, as rental properties.

Rehabbing

"Wisely, and slow. They stumble that run fast."
—William Shakespeare

We've all heard of people who buy a wreck of a house in a great neighborhood, fix it up themselves while living in it, and then sell it for a tidy profit. This assumes the buyers know enough about construction to judge whether a wreck can be saved—whether its foundation, supporting walls and roof beams are sound.

These people also must be able to estimate accurately the costs of supplies and labor. In these projects, rehabbing costs can quickly spiral out of control. More than once, I've heard rehabbers lament that it would have been cheaper to build from bare ground than renovate their existing house.

Common sense must rule whenever you consider a rehab for profit. However, common sense is easier to have about other people's property than your own. Most of us have a blind spot when it comes to fixing up our own property. We simply don't foresee how much work is involved, how long it will take, how much it will cost, and perhaps most dangerous of all, how we tend to keep changing our plans continually.

You probably know at least one couple whose home is a permanent construction site. They didn't know what they were getting into. Now they work weekends and several nights a week after their daytime jobs. Whether they have the energy, and are still speaking to one another, is another matter!

Progress is painfully slow. At times, they run out of money for supplies, which cost far more than they had planned for, so work stops temporarily. Add in the inevitable mistakes and revised plans, and two years' of nonstop construction just fly by. They can hardly remember what it felt like not to be covered in fine dust.

Don't do this to yourself! One way to avoid this self-deceptive, self-indulgent trap is to imagine that you are working for someone else when planning and making estimates. For example, would you promise a client that you could complete a certain project in a certain timeframe at a certain "not to exceed" cost? If not, don't make that same promise to yourself. Make sure to put down all your plans in writing. Then, be sure you have price estimates for labor and supplies before you begin—and stick to them. If your plans became more grandiose as work proceeds, make sure you understand the amount of additional time and expense that's required. And by all means, be sure you have all your permits, approvals and insurance in place before you start anything.

Always follow the contractor's golden rule: Multiply all time and cost estimates by two.

*   *   *

You can also buy fixer-upper homes as an investment strategy, using your existing home's equity to buy or secure a short-term loan. Before you pick up that hammer, though, you need to answer the following questions:

- By how much will your renovations increase the value of the house?
- Can you realistically estimate renovation costs and time?
- How much work can you do yourself? How much will require hired labor?

- Can you finance all the costs involved?

- Do you have enough money to hold the property if it doesn't sell right away?

- Do you know a construction expert whose opinion you can trust?

If you're certain that rehabbing for profit is a promising route to follow, then don't hesitate. Get your Realtor on the phone and start searching for fixer-uppers. Just make sure you use a very sharp pencil as you prepare your budget to fund your project. Here's an example of how such an investment might work:

In a neighborhood where houses sell for $200,000, you buy a rundown property for $150,000. You estimate that it will cost $20,000 and take three months to bring the house in line with neighboring properties. (Remember, as a rehabber you have no ambition to create a dream house. Get in, get it fixed, and get out!)

You put down $7,500 (5 percent) of the purchase price, get a 30-year mortgage loan at 5.75 percent for the $142,500 balance, and pay $5,000 in closing costs. To finance the renovation, you use your existing home equity credit line. Your monthly mortgage payment is $831.59; with taxes and insurance included, it would probably be about $1,100. Let's use that number.

Because you finish the work on time and on budget, your outstanding Realtor resells the house just four months after you bought it; the house fetches $200,000. At settlement, you pay the agent's standard 6 percent commission of $12,000, and we'll say your selling costs were $2,500. What profit do you take away from this deal?

Sold for:	$200,000
Commission:	– 12,000
Net of Sale:	$188,000
Closing Costs:	– 7,500
Purchased for:	– 150,000
Renovation:	– 20,000
Mortgage Payments:	– 4,400
Balance:	$6,100

Four-Month ROI: 19.1%

In the above example, you invested $31,900 and made $6,100 after all expenses were accounted for. You made 19 percent on your money in four months. Of course, there are tax considerations, both pro and con, to consider, but on balance, this was a good investment.

You have to balance whether the money, time and effort you plan to invest in rehabbing will be reflected in an increase in house price. It can be dispiriting to do extensive work, only to see a neighbor's neglected property appreciate by the same amount as yours, simply because market supply, or neighborhood desirability, are the factors controlling house prices.

That said, cosmetic improvements are usually worth doing. A fresh coat of paint inside and outside works wonders for a house. If you have a yard, a few new plantings and some weed killer on the lawn can create a great first impression. If your yard is mostly concrete, a few plants in large pots or tubs can dispel the bareness (so long as you remember to water them).

For additional, practical and financial details on renovation, see Chapter 7.

4

Choosing a Location, Property and Agent

Now that you are determined to take action, and have decided what kind of property you want, location and affordable price are your next concerns. You can save yourself many hours of searching by going to a real estate agent at this point. Agents know what properties are available, along with price ranges and neighborhood desirability.

A Realtor can help you best if you know what you want. Going to a real estate agent without knowing your preferences and requirements is almost asking to be steered to what the agent most wants to get rid of. Agents always have less desirable properties to offer to undiscriminating people. You don't want them guiding you where they want you to go. People who don't know what they want are rarely satisfied by what they get, even when it is a bargain.

Location

We've all heard the expression, "location, location, location." In real estate, location can mean several things. For example, a store at a busy intersection has a more valuable location than one in mid-block on a residential street. However, a condo at a noisy intersection is far less desirable than one in mid-block on a residential street.

Location also refers to the neighborhood. All the properties in a neighborhood undergoing gentrification—that's economist-speak meaning a comeback from hard times—are likely to rise in value, regardless of their site or condition. However, the rate of gentrification is rarely something you can depend on. Investors may have to own a house for more than a decade, as the neighborhood quite definitely, but only very slowly, improves.

You may feel more confident about investing in one neighborhood and less so in another. Follow your instincts. Things such as whether you intend to live in the property, and if so, whether you have school-age children, will influence your decision. Settle these questions ahead of time rather than involve your real estate agent. Remember, too, that the factors influencing your choice of location will probably vary as we analyze the four kinds of properties—first home, trade-up home, vacation home, and rental property—that we are considering as real estate investment opportunities.

Many of us know our own neighborhoods in great detail, but can hardly find our way around an adjoining community. Naturally, the places we know best are where we, and our family and friends, have chosen to live, work and play. We may not have the time or curiosity to see other places.

We may not even be aware of how little we know about the town where we live. You've probably heard people say, "The last time I was out here, it was just a field." Indeed, large tracts of housing seem to come into existence almost overnight! You may need to expand your horizons by doing some exploration. A real estate agent can be a big help here.

Once agents know their clients' preferences and what they can afford, they can simplify the search process by ruling out neighborhoods that are too upscale or downscale. They know which trendy areas have passed their peak and which ones are still ripe for investment. They also know why prices seem inexplicably low in some areas, for reasons such as local pollution, highway planning, criminal activity or political corruption. Your real estate agent can be a unique source for many kinds of knowledge.

When your Realtor sees that you have a clear target in mind and are determined to achieve it, he or she won't waste your time showing you less desirable properties. Competent agents quickly "get it" when you know what you want. Your own attitude has everything to do with how real estate professionals treat you.

Finding a *Good* Real Estate Agent

Finding real estate agents is no problem. Their "FOR SALE" and "SOLD" signs are everywhere. Their ads are on TV. The newspapers are loaded with them. Anyone who has ever bought or sold real estate has probably used one. But the question remains: How can you tell the really good ones from the rest of the bunch?

For me, a top-notch real estate agent is hardworking *and* has truly in-depth knowledge of the local area—facts that he or she knows but the others don't (or don't realize why such things should matter). Furthermore, that agent knows how to apply this wisdom to my particular set of circumstances to deliver what I want. This, by the way, is the winning formula used by every top-producing real estate agent I've ever known.

When I first started, I used real estate agents as simple door openers to see houses. I followed them in my car rather than ride with them, just to keep my independence. I missed a lot, because even a good real estate agent's small talk while driving can be a great help to you. While there are some bad agents, the majority are dedicated and reliable.

Agents are an indispensable source of information on property opportunities. Have them work for you. The more properties you see, the better idea you will have of what's on the market and the more ready you will be to act when you see a good deal.

Contrary to what you might hear, the vast majority of agents don't make big bucks. They are self-employed subcontractors who are affiliated with a broker, and they need a license to practice. Most real estate agents work for commissions (which are paid by the seller at settlement), and if they don't sell houses, or find buyers, they don't make any money.

Here's how a typical commission structure works:

The commission goes to the brokerages where the agents are employed, *not to the agents*. (The seller's broker splits the commission with the broker whose agent found the buyer.) The brokerage then deducts part of the agents' earnings to help pay the lease, support the office and fund advertising and marketing programs. Then, finally, the agent gets paid.

The total average commission paid to the brokers has been hovering at about 5 percent of the actual sale price. When all is said and done, real estate agents make, on average, less than $50,000 a year, according to Real Trend, an industry data warehouse. And take it from me, they work hard for the money!

Service levels can be affected by the kind of brokerage company with which agents are associated, too. There are three types of brokerages:

- **Traditional brokerage companies.** Here's where you'll find the independent real estate agents in your community. Traditional brokers restrict their activities to brokerage, and thus the agents associated with them are free to refer you to lenders and service providers of their own choosing.

- **Real estate services companies.** If you want professional advice and full service in a one-stop shopping arrangement, an agent who works with a real estate services company may have more to offer you. The majority of these companies belong to a national franchise, such as Century 21. Their agents have the freedom to make independent referrals, just like agents who work with traditional brokerage companies.

- **Agent service bureaus.** Agents pay fees rather than percentages of their commissions in this arrangement, and thus favor higher priced properties to cover their costs. RE/MAX is the biggest franchise in this area.

No matter which brokerage you choose, finding an agent with extensive local knowledge and contacts is more important to you than where he or she works.

Buyer's Agent

Here's another important point: "Your" real estate agent may be working hard to put together a transaction that's acceptable, first and foremost, to the seller, then to you. Why? Because that's who ultimately pays the commission. However, even though "your" agent is not necessarily neutral, this does not make the agent your adversary.

If you want an agent who works exclusively for you when you're buying property, you want a so-called "buyer's agent." As the name suggests, a buyer's agent represents only your interests. In these arrangements, you are bound contractually to that agent. Either you can pay your buyer's agent commission yourself, or you can negotiate to have the seller pay it. No fee is set by law, so it is completely negotiable. But it is illegal for buyer's agents to be paid twice in the same deal, so be sure to include in your contract that payment comes either from you or from the seller. As long as you know what you want, and let your real estate agent know what you want, and keep your demands reasonable, you will achieve your goals. The more you understand your own requirements and communicate them, the more readily a real estate agent can find you an ideal property. As in visiting any professional, whether it be a lawyer, doctor or real estate agent, the more you know beforehand, the more you can benefit from professional advice.

What Should a Real Estate Agent Do for You?

"The art of being wise is the art of knowing what to overlook."

—William James

You've made up you're mind—you're going to buy! You know what kind of property you want; you know what kind of neighborhood you want; you've put together a clear picture of your financial affairs; and you've met a real estate agent who strikes you as honest, knowledgeable and hardworking.

Now you must let the agent show you how to benefit from his or her professional expertise. A good agent will steer you to your goal in many ways.

What Can You Afford?

Are you employed full time or part time? Is your spouse or partner employed and involved in the transaction? How much do you earn and how much do you owe? How much can you comfortably pay monthly on a mortgage? Agents who ask these questions are not being nosey and intrusive. They need to be able to select properties at a price level for which you are an acceptable risk. They know what credit lenders will be willing to extend to someone in your financial state. Agents can give you a realistic view of what kinds of properties you are likely to get a mortgage for.

What's the Market Like?

Real estate prices everywhere are affected by mortgage rates. However, prices are also affected by how many homes are on the market, whether sales are brisk or slow, if any new home construction is starting, and other factors with which every good agent is familiar. These agents also know the pros and cons of different neighborhoods and can give you compelling reasons why you should, or should not, consider particular areas. Finally, competent agents know what local properties have been selling for very recently, how long the properties stayed on the market before being sold, and how many are being sold each week.

Doing a Property Search

In a **traditional property search**, an agent drives you from house to house until you found one that was right for you. **Online listings** have taken much of the driving and legwork out of this.

You can get valuable feedback from agents by initially showing them printouts of online property listings that appeal to you, regardless of their locations. Agents can tell you how much to expect to pay for such a property locally, in what neighborhoods they are most likely to be found, and how many are currently on the market.

Negotiation

When you find a property to buy, rely upon your agent's negotiating skills as well as your own. Agents know what concessions to ask for. Price is the obvious thing that most people want to negotiate, but in such narrowly focused discussions, they often overlooking more easily obtainable and even more valuable concessions. Consider negotiating financing terms, date of possession, repair or replacement of damaged items, and inclusion of furniture, appliances, draperies or other costly items.

Due Diligence

Before finalizing a purchase, you need to make your own efforts to ensure that all is well with the property. This is known as due diligence. Your investigation must be centered on two fronts: the property title and the physical condition of the building.

To check out the structure, hire a professional that's certified by the American Society of Home Inspectors (ASHI), www.ashi.org. Their representatives follow recognized guidelines. A routine inspection and final report costs from $200 to $500 in most places. Most important, NEVER assume that any house is sound until it's been thoroughly inspected, *even if it's brand new*! Be sure your agent includes "bail out" language in your offer to protect you in case a serious problem develops. Most sellers will readily agree to repair minor items.

You'll also want to ensure that the deeds to the house and land are "clean," which calls for a title search. Your agent should be able to refer you to a title insurer, or if you prefer, to a real estate lawyer. They will search the public records for claims, tax liens or other impairments regarding the property you want to buy. In some states, you can also find a title insurer yourself and save a few bucks.

In any event, if you're getting a mortgage, the bank will require a clear title and title insurance, which you pay for at settlement. Be aware that title insurance doesn't protect you. It only protects the lender, so I recommend you consider buying additional "owner's title insurance" yourself. The cost is reasonable and it will protect your equity from a previous owner's or lien holder's sudden claim. They do pop up, albeit very rarely.

Seeing Things Differently

"There are two good things in life—freedom of thought
and freedom of action."

—W. Somerset Maugham

When you are not involved in a community, you can pass through
without noticing anything. Some people allow their whole lives to
pass by in this way, seeking only the route of least discomfort.

Deciding to buy real estate, deciding where to buy, and estimat-
ing what you can afford changes your relationship to the world
around you. Working with a real estate agent almost guarantees that
you will never pass through neighborhoods again without noticing
them. They are no longer meaningless collections of houses—they
are now neighborhoods you could, or could not afford, or could do
better than. Your surroundings take on new meaning because you
yourself have changed. Like a chain reaction, perceiving new things
causes further personal change.

I can't predict what courses you will follow or where random
happenings are likely to take you. You need to follow your own nat-
ural inclinations and talents. Each person makes a unique journey.
The way you word your thoughts can affect the outcome of your
thinking. If you persistently ask yourself *why*, you may finally get an
answer. If you persistently ask *how*, you may finally get an even better answer—one that enables you to take action to make changes.
And you have to be ready to move when you see what you want.

I've met too many people who put all their energy into avoiding
pain instead of seeking fulfillment. This is what procrastinators
do—they stay away from risk, see change as a bad thing and stay
hidden safely inside their comfort zones. They delay and delay until
their discomfort level becomes unbearable. When they have no
choice, only then do they decide to take some frantic action that's
almost guaranteed to fall short.

Don't be distracted by economic reports, demographics, housing inventories, data on housing starts and the like. Some people fill their minds with technical reports and jargon, and miss what's in front of their noses. Such information can be of great value to specialists, but in general, it frightens or confuses more people than it helps. Use your real estate agent as a filter for such information. Stick with what you see and can understand. Keep in mind that when something makes sense to you, you may be right; and when it doesn't, you may also be right.

PART II
THE BASICS

5

How to Boost Your Credit Rating and Qualify for a Mortgage

With good credit, you can do anything. You can get the lowest available interest rates on mortgage loans and put down the smallest possible down payment, or no cash at all, on a property you want to purchase. When lenders consider you a low risk, they compete to loan you money.

Lenders use several factors to estimate the risk of advancing a loan to you. Your credit report and credit score are two of the most influential items a loan officer studies when deciding what kind of credit risk you are.

Like a baseball batting average or a golf handicap, your credit score conveys a lot of information in a few digits. The credit scoring system is known as the FICO score, for the Fair Isaac Company that developed it.

Your FICO score ranges from 300 to 950, with higher scores indicating lower risk. If your credit score is at least 580, you can improve it and qualify for a mortgage loan. If it is below 580, you may be beyond help. You can get almost anything you want with a credit score of 700 or higher.

Your debt and payment histories for credit cards, car loans, and the like affect your credit score. So do tax liens, judgments against you, foreclosures and bankruptcy. Major purchases on credit, such as an expensive new car, lower your score.

Three nationwide credit bureaus assign scores: TransUnion, Equifax and Experian. Your score may vary somewhat from one credit bureau to another, but they'll be close enough to give a clear picture of your creditworthiness.

Clear Your Credit Report and Raise Your Credit Score

Your finances are like your body. Take good care of your credit and you'll be rewarded with excellent financial health. Real estate is the most reliable way to achieve long-lived financial health. However, as with physical health, you have to stay active and do the right things.

That's why, when you have problems in your credit report that lower your credit score, you must deal with them before approaching a lender. In other words, you have to make sure you'll qualify for a mortgage loan before asking for one.

According to a 2004 study by the U.S. Public Interest Research Group (PIRG), one in every four credit reports contains errors serious enough to cause your application for a mortgage loan to be rejected. Don't assume that long-ago disputes with a store, credit card company or the doctor's billing department have been cleared up. You may be in for a rude awakening. It is up to you to do your homework to uncover and correct such errors. There is really no excuse for having a bad credit rating due to someone else's negligence.

Then again, some of my clients have deliberately snubbed their noses at creditors, or chosen to ignore calls and letters from collection agencies. They thought that these pests would get the hint and just go away. Huge mistake! These kinds of things haunt you for years. If there's anything derogatory on your credit report that is less than a year old, your loan application is dead on arrival. More than a year old is still very serious, but usually not deadly. Either way, these problems must be cleared up as soon as possible.

You may think that some of the unfavorable things on your credit report are minor, involving sums as small as a few dollars, and that lenders will look the other way at such trivial matters. Some may, but many won't. That's why you must clear away all of them. Get started by contacting the three credit bureaus listed below and requesting a copy of your credit report. By law, you're entitled to one free copy of your credit report annually. (They'll charge you a fee for your credit *score*, however.) Follow their procedures for correcting errors.

TransUnion
800-916-8800
www.transunion.com

Equifax
800-685-1111
www.equifax.com

Experian
888-397-3742
www.experian.com

You can also call 877-322-8228 or go to www.annualcreditreport.com to request all three credit reports from one place. This is the official agency for dispensing credit reports on behalf of the three credit bureaus.

To file a complaint against a credit bureau, contact the Federal Trade Commission at 877-382-4357 or go to the agency's Web page at www.ftc.gov. To find a lawyer who specializes in this area, contact the National Association of Consumer Advocates at 202-452-1989 or go to the organization's Web page: www.naca.net.

Be prepared to contact the firms or individuals who reported your transgressions. This may be difficult, but it is critical to your future. This is not the time for pride, emotions, temper or demands. You are in the wrong and you must approach these matters in a calm, businesslike way.

If you have to, go from person to person within a company. Make call after call. Admit that you made a mistake and sincerely apologize. Ask to negotiate a settlement and to receive a signed release on letterhead, explaining that the company or person is satisfied with the settlement. Then send copies of the release to the credit bureaus to have the blot removed from your credit record.

If your problem involved a credit card company, call and ask them for similar consideration and a release letter once any stains have been cleared up. When you receive the letter, send it to the three credit bureaus immediately. (By the way, when it comes to the credit bureaus, always communicate in threes.)

Credit bureaus must correct your report, usually within 30 days. Be careful never to accidentally dispute an item that has been dropped, because this will cause it to be reinstated and it could reappear on your credit report.

Contact the bureaus every time you spot an unfamiliar inquiry or record of unusual activity. Ask for the names and addresses of the parties associated with them. When the bureau identifies the parties responsible, contact them and request that the items be removed.

This can be a lot of work, and you may be tempted to call a credit repair agency to clean up your credit report. *I strongly advise against this.* Many such agencies charge hundreds of dollars, yet deliver little or nothing in the way of a better credit rating. Save your money. Make the effort and do the job yourself.

Close Down Your Credit Cards

The more credit you have available, the greater the likelihood that you'll go further into debt once you receive your mortgage loan. And the more debt you assume, the higher your risk of nonrepayment, and the worse your credit score becomes. Sounds like *Catch-22*, doesn't it?

The solution is simple: Close all your credit card accounts except for the one or two that are essential. Such a radical step will substantially lessen your available credit, thus raising your credit score. However, before closing down the accounts, make sure none of them have balances exceeding 75 percent of each one's available credit line. Why? Because card balances exceeding 75 percent of your available credit are held against you whether the account is open or not.

The good news is that, once you get under the magic 75-percent threshold, your credit rating goes up. So, if you have to, rob MasterCard to pay Visa and get all your cards below 75 percent of available credit.

For the few surviving accounts you intend to keep open, call those credit card companies and ask for a lower rate, saying you want to stay with them. You may or may not get it, but you have nothing to lose but higher interest.

Clearing Up Negative Mortgage Information

You may have unfavorable items to clear in your credit report regarding payments on a previous mortgage, or on the one you already hold if you're refinancing or investing.

Fixing mortgage problems can occasionally be dicey. The lender may have difficulty finding your mortgage because the note was sold to another lender, and your records and initial ID number have been lost. Ask if the mortgage was sold and if a new ID number was assigned on purchase.

Lenders score mortgages by the day payments are made. If you haven't always paid on time, it may or may not be on your credit report. If it is not on the report, don't mention it. On the other hand, you may have made your payments on time but find that, according to your credit report, you didn't. Get the lender to correct the company records, and send you written verification that the matter has been resolved. Again, contact the "big three" credit bureaus with this new information.

Bankruptcies and Foreclosures

Although a traditional lender will not lend to anyone with a bankruptcy a year or two old, it is possible to get a mortgage loan six months after a foreclosure, or once you've been discharged in a Chapter 7 bankruptcy. Nevertheless, both bankruptcies and foreclosures are the most difficult and vexing obstacles to overcome as far as credit ratings are concerned.

Dispute the Unfixable

You may not be able to do much about removing a foreclosure, bankruptcy or other major stain from your credit report, but you can dispute them to your advantage. Disputing such items freezes them and keeps them from burying your credit score.

Just before applying for a mortgage loan, dispute all major unfavorable items at all three bureaus. Credit bureaus then will have 30 days to respond. Then, 25 days later, go back and dispute everything again. This will "renew" your dispute and should keep your credit score at a quasi-acceptable level long enough for you to get your mortgage.

Items older than two years should not be disputed. The older an item is, the less it affects your credit rating. But if you dispute it, you reactivate it and run the risk that it will reappear as a "fresh" derogatory item on your report.

Sometimes, it helps to attach a letter of explanation to older major items. One of my clients confessed that he'd broken a lease during a bitter divorce. Later, in good faith, he agreed to make restitution for his half of the remaining rent to the apartment company. The manager initially agreed, but tried to intimidate him for the full amount once his half was paid. He refused to pay further, so the management company reported him as a deadbeat.

In spite of this, three years later I suggested that he explain the circumstances to his mortgage lender. Initially skeptical, the lender was impressed with his sincerity and his willingness to own up to his actions. Lo and behold, my client closed on a conventional 30-year, fixed-rate loan at 6 percent two weeks later. Bubble proofing strikes again!

If you have a reasonable explanation for why there's a bad entry on your report (other than forgetfulness or neglect), put it in writing and have the credit bureaus include it in your credit report. You never know.

When Lenders Request Your Credit Report

When lenders request your credit report and credit score, it triggers a blinking yellow caution light to future potential lenders that you are trying to borrow money. To them, you become a higher potential risk. Five hits from lenders reduce your credit score by one point, and six hits by two. Your inquiries about your own score do not affect it.

When One Partner Has Poor Credit

If one partner in a couple seeking to qualify for a mortgage loan has poor credit, he or she should not seek to be listed. Instead, the partner on record can make a separate agreement with the less creditworthy partner that once the latter makes 36 monthly payments on time, he or she gets to be a 50/50 partner in the property, with their name listed on mortgage and so forth.

Creating a Credit Rating

Never having assumed debt, and therefore never having repaid it, doesn't make you a stellar applicant for a loan. It means that you are an unknown quantity in the credit world, and a potentially high risk. You need a track record of borrowing wisely and repaying on time.

To create a suitable record, find a credit card with a low ceiling of, say, $500. Charge a good portion of your limit in a month, and pay it all back when your statement arrives.

Do that for two months and your ceiling will be raised to $1,000. Do it for three more months and your ceiling will be $5,000. You now have an excellent credit report and high credit score.

(You will find more inside information and tips on my CD, *Credit Repair Secrets*.)

Qualifying for a Mortgage Loan

Once you have cleaned up your credit report and boosted your credit score as much as you can, allow at least 30 days for the credit bureaus to make changes. After that time, check to see that all three bureaus have complied. If they haven't, call and find out why, and ask them again to make the changes. It is bothersome, but necessary, because you must qualify for a loan.

If the credit bureaus have made the changes, for a modest fee you can request your credit scores. Your scores will allow you to estimate how lenders are going to view you. How would you, as a lender, assess the risk of someone with a credit report and score like yours?

Risk is what lenders focus on. The more risk you present to lenders, the higher the interest rate on a loan. If lenders see you as a low-risk borrower, they will compete to give you a loan by lowering their interest rates. The better you qualify for a mortgage loan, the stronger your position will be when you actually seek the loan.

Along with your credit report and credit score, lenders will also look closely at these three factors:

- **Debt-to-income ratio**
- **Expense-to-income ratio**
- **Income sources**

Your **debt-to-income ratio** compares your total monthly financial obligations, including your current housing arrangement, with your monthly gross income. Ideally, your monthly payments should be 36 percent or less of your monthly income. However, you can qualify for certain low down payment, higher-interest mortgages even if you do not have an optimal debt-to-income ratio.

Your **expense-to-income** ratio compares your monthly housing expenses to your monthly gross income. Your monthly housing expenses include your rent or mortgage payment, and any mortgage insurance, hazard insurance, property taxes and homeowner's fees you pay. In traditional, 20-percent-down mortgages, such expenses should be 28 percent or less of your monthly income. If you are putting down less, however, your lender will lower your E-to-I ratio (to, say, 25 percent).

Your **income sources** should be stable and dependable—this is music to a lender's ears. Lenders will also want to know how long you have held your present job and how long you can reasonably expect to hold it. They want to be reassured that you will continue earning at least as much as you do today.

Note: If your income is seasonal, or if you work on commission or are self-employed, you might not be suited for a traditional mortgage, but don't be alarmed. Today, mortgage lenders have a wide variety of alternatives for which you can qualify.

What Can You Afford?

The traditional fixed-interest, 30-year mortgage is still the most popular, but many people today can get mortgages that require little or no cash at settlement.

Relaxing the demand for a big, upfront deposit has put previously unattainable houses within the reach of cash-poor purchasers. But, these mortgages can sometimes make it much more difficult to estimate what you can afford. The final amount of your loan also will depend, to some extent, on your newfound personal qualities of perseverance, determination and thoroughness. Qualifying for the best mortgage is a perfect test for character building, as we discussed in the early chapters. Have no doubt that in the nitty-gritty real estate world, you will be tested many times in unpredictable ways. And you'll rise to the occasion at every opportunity, by working your *Bubble Proof* techniques.

However, this doesn't translate into *carte blanche* for you to go after the biggest, gaudiest mortgage you can imagine! Loans still turn, first and foremost, on creditworthiness—no matter how industrious and virtuous an applicant might be. Remember that realistic expectations are just as laudable as integrity.

Any banker or mortgage company would be happy to help you estimate how much house you can afford—but get ready for a full-court press from the sales department while you're there. Some people don't mind, but others recoil at the idea. If you're in the latter category, the best place to go is the Internet. You'll find Web sites and calculators galore, for all kinds of potential loans and many conceivable scenarios.

Thanks to its impartiality, the best Web page I've found is the one maintained by the federal agency known as the Government National Mortgage Association—Ginnie Mae for short—at www.ginniemae.gov. Here you can use a mortgage affordability calculator, a rent-versus-buy calculator, and read generous amounts of excellent advice about first-time buying as well as long-term real estate investing.

The Ginnie Mae Web site suggests how to list your income, savings, monthly expenses and debt. You enter these four total amounts into the online affordability calculator to help you determine how much real estate you can afford. What you receive are estimates, calculated from national averages, with the assumption that the borrower is married with two dependents. Data is given for three kinds of loans, and more-detailed estimates are available.

Finding a Lender

Someone buying a new home needs to find someone willing to advance a mortgage loan at a competitive interest rate. But, since you're not only buying but also planning to be a real estate investor, it is important for you to find a lender who supports what you are doing today and values you as a future repeat customer.

Such people can be easier to find than you might expect. To make money, lenders have to advance loans, and if you qualify for thousands today, and honor your commitments to pay your loan back on time, you'll potentially qualify for millions in the future.

More often than not, your character and self-knowledge will help put your loan application over the top. A loan officer who has that fabled "good feeling" about you will probably give your loan a green light, even if it means a half-percent less for the bank. Lenders bet on people as much as they do on their financial data.

Your real estate agent or broker is another rich source of referrals to lenders. They know which banks and lenders have the best rates, shortest turnaround time, most flexible requirements and the most competent staffs. And don't overlook your colleagues at work and people in your community—they may have suggestions and even connections to mortgage makers. Such personal referrals are often the most reliable.

Since rates and terms vary from place to place, often by surprising degrees, I urge you to visit at least three lenders. And don't hesitate to tell one source that you've gotten the same deal, or even a better one, from the one down the street. Competition for your business always works in your favor, and will often compel a lender to make a sweetened counteroffer.

I'll end this chapter with an overview of the kinds of records and documents most lenders will need to see, regardless of which mortgage product you decide on.

Borrower documents likely to speed the lending process

Bring the following documents with you when you meet the lender, but never show your income tax return or other documents unless specifically requested. Lenders can't ignore documents you show them, even if they want to.

Bank statements
IRA statements
Savings account statements
Stocks statements
Bonds statements
Certificates of deposit
Trust fund statements
Pay stubs for past two months
Tax returns for past two years
Current loan statements
Leases or rental agreements
Deposit verification
Other sources of income
Relationship verification
Divorce records
Bankruptcy records

6

What Kind of Mortgage Is Right for You?

A mortgage is a loan you take out on a property and then repay, usually monthly, over a specified span of years. Your monthly payment is allocated to repay interest and principal in what is called an amortization schedule.

Your lender provides this schedule. It shows how your payments break down over the life of the loan. At first, most of your payments will go to paying the interest on the mortgage, and only a small fraction will go to paying back the principal. As time passes, the percentage of principal paid increases, while the percentage of interest decreases. By paying back the principal, the owner builds equity in the property.

Although most mortgages today are still of the traditional 30-year, fixed-rate variety, lenders now offer an array of specialized alternatives. Before looking at these many options, let's briefly examine the three main kinds of mortgages you are likely to be offered: **fixed rate**, **adjustable rate** and **balloon**.

Fixed-Rate Mortgages

The traditional 30-year, fixed-rate mortgage usually has the lowest monthly payment over the life of the loan. Homeowners enjoy their predictability since the rate is locked. Lenders also offer fixed-rate mortgages for 10, 15 or 20 years at somewhat lower interest rates, but higher monthly payments. If you can make the higher payments, I think a shorter-term loan is usually best: You pay less interest in the long run, and build equity faster. Just be realistic when you gauge your ability to handle higher monthly payments.

Adjustable-Rate Mortgages (ARMs)

A typical adjustable-rate mortgage, or ARM, has two components: a fixed rate of interest, and an adjustable rate. The popular 3/1 ARM, for example, has a fixed rate of interest for three years, followed by a second term in which the interest rate is adjusted once a year for the remaining years of the mortgage. ARMs are available in many versions, such as 10/1, 7/1, and 5/1 to name just a few.

The adjustable rate is tied to a popular *index,* such as the prime rate or a Treasury bond rate, and the rate has a *margin* of, say, 2 percent. So, if the prime rate is 5 percent when your ARM is first adjusted, and it has a margin of two, you'll pay 7 percent interest for the next 12 months. Then, another rate change occurs.

ARMs also contain a so-called *rate cap*. This cap holds a rate change to predetermined limits of, say, no more than two percentage points' worth of increase (or decrease—rates can also fall) per year. A *lifetime cap* states the maximum amount that interest may rise over the life of the loan. Nor can the adjustable interest drop beneath a pre-agreed floor.

Interest rates for the initial term are generally a percent or two lower than fixed-rate mortgages. This means that your initial payments will be less, so you may qualify for a larger mortgage amount.

Many first-time buyers choose an ARM with the goal of refinancing before the adjustable-rate term begins. With this in mind, lenders offer an increasing number of convertible features for ARM loans. Among the most attractive is the option of converting to a fixed-rate loan after a certain time.

In addition, ARMs can make properties affordable that might not be affordable at fixed rates. Investors often use ARMs to purchase rental property for less, because they can raise rents to cover their increased costs once the ARM rate adjusts upward.

Here, a word of caution. Some buyers, dazzled by these products' low initial interest rates, take out an ARM without regard for the possible financial consequences later on. Be advised: Once ARMs start to recalibrate, the increases in your monthly payments can be startling. Never take out any kind of an ARM with the idea that you'll simply handle those higher payments down the road. "Crossing that bridge when I come to it" is not a strategy for financial well-being. Bubble proof your ARM application by determining if you would be able to manage a higher payment *today*.

Balloon Mortgages

Balloon mortgages have fixed-rate, monthly payments based on a 30-year amortization schedule, but there's a twist. At the end of their five- or seven-year term, the entire loan balance must be paid off. Thus the term "balloon."

These mortgages are designed for real estate investors and homeowners who don't expect to hold a property for more than their five- or seven-year terms. Designated by the numbers 5/25 or 7/23, balloon mortgages have lower interest rates and lower credit requirements than either traditional fixed-rate or ARM loans. Most balloon mortgages also have a reset option that permits the borrower, at the end of the five- or seven-year term, to refinance the balance due at prevailing market rates.

You must have a plan of action before taking out a balloon loan. Remember that if you can't pay off the balance on your note by the end of the balloon's term, by either refinancing or selling, you may face foreclosure. Balloon mortgages are not loans for people who want to forget about real estate once they have bought a home they like. You don't get to sit in a rocking chair on the porch for the next 30 years with a balloon loan.

Mortgage Insurance

If you don't put at least 20 percent down at closing, you'll probably be required by your lender to buy private mortgage insurance, commonly called PMI. PMI covers the extra amount the bank lends when down payments are less that 20 percent of the home's loan-to-value ratio. In case you default on your mortgage, the bank is reimbursed for the shortfall. The "upside" is that the bank is more inclined to make a loan where buyers only put down 3, 5 or 10 percent of a property's price tag.

PMI isn't cheap—depending on your location, it can cost from one-half to 1 percent of your loan amount annually. Additionally, you cannot deduct mortgage insurance on your taxes. However, once your equity stake hits 22 percent, federal law requires PMI to be canceled.

Finding the Right Mortgage

Many first-time borrowers are surprised when they discover that the bank giving them their mortgage does not intend to retain ownership of it.

These days, the vast majority of mortgage money is actually provided by a collection of government-backed companies or agencies.

They are in the business of purchasing mortgages from banks and, in effect, guaranteeing that the mortgages will be paid by the borrowers.

The Federal National Mortgage Association ("Fannie Mae" for short) and the Federal Home Loan Mortgage Corporation ("Freddie Mac") are federally chartered, private companies that purchase mortgages from lenders. The firms then use the mortgages to back securities that they sell on the capital markets. These investment-grade products allow the agencies to plow mortgage money back to approved lenders.

Their loan guarantees are for relatively modest amounts that middle- and upper-middle-class buyers need. Loans for higher amounts, needed by upper-class and wealthy homebuyers, must still come from private lenders without government backing. In such cases, these loans are often called jumbo mortgages.

The Federal Housing Administration (FHA) and Veterans Administration (VA) also back mortgages. In the next few pages, we will look at all these mortgage types, and some others.

*   *   *

"Let's see what's available before we decide what we want," some people say—only to emerge from reviewing mortgages more confused than when they started.

Trying to understand all the different mortgage types can be like reading an extensive menu. If you have absolutely no idea what you want to eat when entering a restaurant, looking at a long, involved menu might not be much help. But if you know you want to eat fish, for instance, the menu is greatly simplified.

Likewise, if you know what you want as a homebuyer or investor, you can quickly set aside the mortgages that are not for you and select the ones that satisfy your needs. You may not find a *perfect* mortgage, but you will find one that enables you to purchase the property you want.

Fannie Mae Mortgages (www.fanniemae.com)

Freddie Mac Mortgages (www.freddiemac.com)

Fannie Mae is America's largest source of financing for home mortgages, and the largest nonbank financial services company in the world. Through its American Dream Commitment, the company seeks to expand first-time homeownership, especially among minorities, and to enlarge the supply of affordable housing where needed.

Freddie Mac also keeps money flowing to mortgage lenders in support of homeownership and rental housing. The company helps to hold down housing costs by providing better access to home financing.

Both Fannie Mae's and Freddie Mac's product lines are extensive. Besides 15-, 20-, 30-, and 40-year fixed-rate mortgages, the firms offer a variety of ARMs, balloons, and innovative loans for energy efficient homes, construction, renovation, second mortgages, rural housing, and even a loan program for borrowers with credit problems.

See their Internet sites for more complete information.

No/Low Down Payment Mortgages

If you have very good credit, but little or no money, these mortgages may be for you. "Low down" loans require as little as a 3-percent payment at settlement, and "no down" loans require no payment. The loans are good for getting creditworthy, cash-poor customers into a long-term loan commitment. However, these products seldom feature the lowest interest rates. And since nearly the entire purchase price is being financed, monthly payments may be stiff.

Jumbo Mortgages

Jumbo mortgages are for well-to-do homebuyers who need to borrow amounts that are larger than Fannie Mae or Freddie Mac are willing to back. Since the originating bank may be required to hold the mortgage and service it for the life of the loan, a "jumbo" generally has a higher interest rate. Some private investment firms, such as Merrill Lynch, will purchase and pool jumbo loans, and use them to back securities that are sold on the capital markets.

FHA Mortgages (www.hud.gov)

If you are short of cash, a Federal Housing Administration (FHA) mortgage—with its low down payment requirement and easier credit qualifications—makes an attractive option.

The FHA insures mortgages for people with low to moderate incomes. (Low income is defined as being between 50 and 80 percent of a given area's median income; moderate income is defined as below 115 percent of an area's median income.) FHA-backed mortgages usually have a fixed rate of interest, although some ARMs are available.

Thanks to the FHA's guaranteeing the loan, borrowers enjoy a lower-than-usual down payment—often just 3 to 5 percent of the purchase price. The guarantee also permits more relaxed credit requirements. However, the amount of the mortgage is likely to be for less too. The amount varies according to regional housing prices.

As with most mortgage commitments where the down payment is less than 20 percent, mortgage insurance is required with FHA mortgages. The premium, divided into twelfths, becomes part of the monthly payments. A 1.5 percent advance on the insurance is part of the closing costs.

VA Mortgages
(www.homeloans.va.gov)

Eligible veterans can benefit from mortgages guaranteed by the Veterans Administration (VA). It is easier to qualify for VA than FHA mortgages, and usually no down payment is required on purchase.

Specialized Mortgages

These options can make borrowing a win/win situation for both you and the lender. Each of the following loan options is described briefly, along with whom the loan might suit best. For example's sake, most of the loans are structured as if their terms were a full 30 years.

The interest rate level offered with each loan is often the lure for borrowers. When you meet with your lender, you'll have to decide whether the interest rate makes the loan's conditions acceptable to you, or whether you'd be willing to pay a higher interest rate for more acceptable loan conditions.

Biweekly Mortgages

This mortgage requires a payment every two weeks. However, since you're making 26 payments a year instead of 12 a year, in effect you're making an additional monthly payment each year and thus paying off your mortgage faster. Biweekly mortgages are a great way to save huge amounts of interest and build equity much faster. This loan, if a newcomer can afford it, is often my number one recommendation for starting down the *Bubble Proof* road on the right foot.

Thirty Due in Seven Mortgage

Here, the interest rate and payments remain fixed for seven years with mortgage. Beginning with the eighth year, the interest rate is changed once—to a previously decided new rate—and then remains unchanged for the rest of the loan. This mortgage is for people who plan to sell the property before seven years, but want a fallback option in case they change their minds. It is also for those who intend to remain beyond seven years and can tolerate one payment adjustment.

Thirty Due in Five Mortgage

This is another version of the same loan. With this mortgage, the interest rate and payments remain fixed for five years. In the sixth year, the interest rate adjusts once, to a predetermined new rate, and then remains the same for the duration of the loan.

One-Year ARM

The interest rate changes every year in a one-year ARM, so that the monthly payment is subject to change every year for the term of the loan. This adjustable-rate mortgage suits borrowers who want the lowest interest rate available in the first year, and are willing to accept probable annual rate and payment increases. Usually they hope to sell the property quickly, or do not qualify for other mortgages.

80/20 Loan

This combination first and second mortgage loan program offers an 80 percent loan-to-value first mortgage (to avoid PMI) and a 20 percent second mortgage, sometimes packaged as a home equity loan. In this 100 percent financing, you make no down payment—but the qualifications are steep and interest rates are higher. If you have excellent credit and make a good living, 80/20 mortgages can be lucrative. They are offered in both traditional or ARM variations.

80/15/5 Loan

This combination first and second mortgage loan program offers an 80 percent loan-to-value first mortgage and a 15 percent second mortgage. You make a down payment of 5 percent at settlement. Similarly, an 80/10/10 loan offers an 80 percent loan-to-value first mortgage and a 10 percent second mortgage. You make a 10 percent down payment.

About Interest-Only Payments and Negative Amortization

Keeping the early mortgage payments as low as possible is a recent concept that has made loans possible for many real estate investors. However, some of these mortgages can cause an unwanted side effect called negative amortization.

In a typical mortgage, your monthly payment does two things: It pays the interest charged by the lender, and gradually pays back the amount borrowed, or principal. For example, in a 30-year, fixed-rate mortgage of $100,000 at 6 percent interest, the monthly payment is $599.55. Making 360 on-time monthly payments would pay off the mortgage in full—interest and principal. It is thus known as a fully amortizing payment.

Of course, larger monthly payments would pay the mortgage in less than 30 years and generate an impressive savings in interest. By the same token, paying less than the amount due each month won't pay back the loan in 30 years—the loan would be only partially amortized and still generating 6 percent interest on the unpaid balance.

To keep early payments as small as possible, and so that borderline applicants can qualify for mortgages, some loans feature interest-only payments, minimum payment options and partial payment choices. These mortgages may *appear* to be borrower-friendly. But remember: All mortgages allot the lion's share of your payment to the interest due in the early years of the loan, and very little goes to repaying the principal.

In other words, if you don't pay enough to cover the interest due, you have a shortfall—which is added to the amount already owed, so that your balance goes up instead of down! This is classic negative amortization, and yes, it can be a very bad situation because you are building absolutely no equity. And if you need to sell, you could wind up owing more that the house is worth.

Negative amortization can be found in some specialized mortgages. For example, there's the **graduated payment mortgage (GPM),** in which negative amortization reduces early payments at the cost of hefty later payments. GPMs differ widely in interest rates, payment amounts and times involved. I only recommend them to clients who'll very likely have bigger salaries in a few years (i.e., doctors, lawyers).

Another kind of negative amortization package is nicknamed the **Pick a Pay Loan.** Pick a pay loans give borrowers a choice of payment amounts, with minimum payments that may be only half the amount of customary payments.

Knowing that they do not have to meet rigidly fixed payment amounts every month can give borrowers the flexibility they need to take out larger mortgages than they otherwise might. The payment menu has three (or sometimes more) levels: 1) a minimum payment, usually involving negative amortization, which is adjusted monthly and capped at 7.5 percent annually; 2) an interest-only payment; and 3) a fully amortizing payment.

Usually, a pick a pay loan's interest rate is based on the Monthly Treasury Average (MTA). That's a rolling index of the past 12 months' bond yields. The term of the loan may be up to 40 years.

These mortgages are useful if, say, you work on commission, you own a business or the bulk of your income is awarded in bonuses. However, they are among the most volatile loans out there. Borrowers could pay dearly if interest rates suddenly spike or their incomes dwindle. With these loans, the watchwords are *caveat emptor*.

Special Needs Mortgages

These days, you can find mortgages if you have special needs. You would probably qualify if your income is low to moderate and you have a disability, or if family members with disabilities live with you.

Another special mortgage is available for Native Americans who purchase a house on tribal lands.

Lease with the Option to Buy

In a lease option, the tenant receives an option to buy the landlord's house or condo, and a portion of a tenant's rent is set aside as a down payment.

Here how it works: Let's say you're renting my $200,000 house for $1,500 a month and you'd like to buy it. I'm motivated to sell, but you only have $5,000 for a down payment—not enough to qualify for an affordable mortgage.

We agree to a lease option instead. I grant you a one-year option to buy my house for $200,000. In exchange, you agree to pay me a new monthly rent of $2,000. Each month, I credit you $500 toward the purchase of my house. You can exercise your option after making 12 on-time payments of $2,000.

At the end of the year, let's say the housing market has fallen. You decide not to buy my house. According to our agreement, I keep the $6,000 in extra rent. You can either vacate or stay, and continue paying rent to me under a new lease agreement.

But if you want to buy the property, you now have $11,000 to put down—your original $5,000, plus the $6,000 you've accrued over the previous 12 months. Now you can qualify for an FHA loan, because you have a 5-percent down payment. And, if the housing market has appreciated over the past year, you've just made an excellent investment.

Seller Financing

Buyers naturally concentrate on price and hope to lower it by whatever means necessary. As a buyer, however, price may not be the most important element in your deal. Getting the financing may be the most important factor, because without that, there is no deal.

If you can't find financing for a deal through lenders, consider seller financing. In this arrangement, the buyer agrees to pay the seller's asking price if the seller finances the deal. These deals are transacted as if a bank was involved, but here the seller is the bank. Once all items are settled, such as interest rates, loan terms, deposit, escrow, insurance and other details, the buyer executes a promissory note and trust deed in the seller's favor.

As a buyer, you'll need to know up front if the owner still has a mortgage on the house, and if so, how much is owed. The unpaid balance will have to be covered before you can buy so that you obtain unencumbered title to the structure and land.

Seller financing can be a boon to buyers. For one thing, there are very few closing costs. Sellers don't charge loan fees (points) and seldom require mortgage insurance. The time it takes to settle is much shorter too. There is very little paperwork involved. And at tax time, you can deduct your interest and taxes just as if a bank had granted your mortgage.

However, a seller must be convinced that the buyer is a good credit risk. He or she will want to see your credit report. Thus, it is a good idea to impress the seller with your creditworthiness—before even suggesting an owner-carried loan.

In addition, don't expect a seller to charge you less interest than he or she would find in other investments, especially in a booming market. In good times, sellers can often get what they ask without making any concessions.

Finally, these deals can become involved. Have your attorney advise you while you're negotiating, and of course, get his or her OK before you sign anything.

All-Inclusive Trust Deed (AITD)

An all-inclusive trust deed (AITD) secures a wraparound loan that incorporates an existing loan with a new loan made by the property seller. The AITD terms, such as rate, maturity date, payment amount, late charges and prepayment penalties are negotiable.

Home Equity Loans and Lines of Credit

Using a credit line to borrow against the equity in your home has become a popular source of consumer credit. Rather than using the so-called frozen equity in your home to buy a more expensive car or go on a cruise, use it to invest in your future by purchasing more real estate. Lenders offer a variety of home equity loans and credit lines. They're essentially second mortgages on your home, so the interest is normally tax deductible. They come either with a fixed or a variable interest rate, and most banks charge one-time upfront fees at closing.

As with any loan, shop around! Some will suit you better than others will. You may have to contact many lenders before finding the credit line best tailored to your needs.

Alternatively, you can allow my company, BackyardLoans.com, to do the legwork for you. BackyardLoans.com has access to hundreds of lenders, can answer questions about the conditions of individual financing, and help you make the right decisions regarding your line of credit.

Home Equity FAQs

Is a home equity loan or credit line right for me?

If you need to borrow, a home equity loan or credit line can provide you with large amounts of cash at relatively low interest rates, along with tax advantages unavailable with other kinds of loans. On the other hand, using your home as collateral for the loan may put it at risk if you can't make the monthly payments. When you sell your home, these loans must be paid off at settlement.

How much can I borrow?

If you have good credit and no major debt, you can probably borrow up to 85 percent of the appraised value of your home. Ask about the length of the loan, and if there is a minimum withdrawal requirement.

How about interest rates?

Interest rates vary, so it is worth checking several lenders for the lowest rate. Be aware that the annual percentage rate (APR) that will be quoted to you is based on interest alone and does not include points or closing costs.

You'll also need to decide whether you want a fixed-rate or variable-rate loan or line of credit. Find out which index (such as the prime rate) the lender bases the interest rate on, and what margin is added for profit. When considering a variable interest rate, check on the rate's periodic cap and lifetime cap. If you are offered a lower introductory interest rate with lower payments, ask how much your later interest rate and payments will rise as a result. Ask if it will be possible at some future time to change from a variable to a fixed rate of interest.

Will I pay upfront closing costs?

You could pay closing costs for such items as application fees, title searches and points. Be sure the loan officer explains all your costs to you before you proceed.

What about continuing costs?

Some lenders require you to pay continuing costs throughout the term of the loan, in addition to closing costs. These costs may include an annual membership or participation fee, due whether you take out a loan or not, and/or a transaction fee every time you borrow money.

What are my rights with this kind of loan?

The Federal Truth in Lending Act requires lenders to inform you about the terms and costs of a loan at the time you are given an application. Lenders must disclose the APR, payment terms, all charges, and variable rate features, as well as giving you a descriptive brochure about home equity loans and lines of credit.

After opening a home equity loan or line of credit, you have three days to cancel it for any reason. You must inform the lender of the cancellation in writing and the lender must return any fees that you have paid. Once the loan or line of credit is open, the lender may not terminate it or change its terms, if you abide by the agreement. However, read the contract very carefully and do not sign any agreement with clauses that you don't understand.

Retirement Accounts

Tax rules have been relaxed to allow first-time homebuyers to borrow from their retirement accounts without incurring the mandated 10 percent penalty. What's more, I've seen cases where it was worthwhile for a real estate investor to borrow from a retirement account, even though it triggered the 10 percent penalty. I'm not necessarily recommending this course of action, though. Before taking anything out of your retirement account, check with your tax advisor first.

A traditional retirement account (IRA) or Roth IRA can enable you to make a down payment or pay closing costs. A 401(k) plan is more complicated, because you are really borrowing from yourself and making payments to your own account. But a relative with a 401(k) can borrow from his or her account and loan you funds, or give you the money as a gift to buy property.

Employer-Assisted Housing (EAH)

Employer-Assisted Housing programs are becoming more popular as companies struggle to attract and keep good workers. Check with your employer to see if it offers EAH incentives. These funds can normally be used toward your down payment or closing costs, and for interest rate buy-downs that lower your monthly mortgage payment.

Home Improvement Loans

You can use these loans to repair or improve a property you already own, or to buy and renovate a property. You can use a Fannie Mae construction-to-permanent mortgage to buy land and construct a building on it.

Government Programs

Your real estate agent and lender should know if you qualify for any federal, state, or local housing programs. For example, the U.S.

Department of Housing and Urban Development (HUD) has programs to encourage teachers and law enforcement officers to become
homeowners, as well as a number of other programs. For local information, visit www.HUD.gov/buying/localbuying or call the agency
at 202-708-1112. Your state, city or community housing authority
can also provide you with information on local housing programs.

Understanding Your Lender

I have asked you to clean up your credit report and raise your credit score for a very good reason: to impress lenders with your creditworthiness. Bankers have to make loans in order to make money
themselves. They want to lend you money, and will do so, providing
you present yourself as a low risk.

Like bankers, mortgage brokers have the same goal—they want
to make mortgages to homebuyers. Brokers usually work for mortgage or consumer finance companies and get a commission of 0.2 to
0.4 percent of each loan they originate. Within a year of issuing a
mortgage, the mortgage company will almost certainly sell it to a
larger mortgage company or Wall Street firm, and pocket another
1.5 percent or so of the loan value in commission.

Here, in a nutshell, is why lenders are so obsessed with getting
to know all about you. Wall Street firms that buy these mortgages in
huge numbers look for specific traits in the people who take out
mortgages. Banks that generate solid mortgages make money from
Wall Street buyers. Mortgage makers who produce shaky loans don't.
That's why, if your credit is strong, your lender will be happy to issue
a mortgage to you. That's the bottom line. They make money by
lending money.

Completing a Mortgage Application

When you're ready to act, it pays to get a prequalification from a mortgage maker. This process is like the pregame warm-up. You sit down with your lender and provide information as if you were applying for an actual mortgage. The lender then prescreens you to see how much money you're likely to qualify for, assuming you have been honest about your finances and that you don't suffer a calamity between now and the time you actually take out a loan.

Having a "prequal" is essential. No real estate agent is going to invest the time and energy it takes showing properties to you if you're a walking question mark. But with a prequalification letter, your agent will know what to show you, and how much leeway there might be to work with. It's the most direct route to the happy ending you're hoping for.

Let's assume that you've found the ideal house. Now the moment of truth has arrived; you apply for the mortgage. This isn't another test run, like with your prequalification. Your loan application is for real this time. Here's what to expect:

Terms and Amounts

Carefully review the terms and amounts in your loan application to make sure they are what you have chosen. Once you have signed the application and it has been accepted, changes may be difficult or impossible to make.

Lock-In Options

Your lender will offer you a variety of lock-in options regarding your interest rate. Locking in your rate can protect you from increases in interest before your mortgage is finalized. You may have to pay points for lock options (a point being 1 percent of the loan amount). Obtain the lock option in writing and make sure its effectiveness extends beyond the closing date of your purchase in case there's a delay.

I advise people not to become obsessed with the interest rate, as so many tend to do. People complain of mortgage interest rates even when they have put little or no money down. They don't realize that they now own a home and its appreciation in value each year puts them way ahead of where they were.

Verification
You can expect your lender to go through much of the same routine as with your prequalification. However, assuming you use the same lender, this time the procedure should be less rigorous.

Expect a re-examination of your credit rating. In addition, you may need to provide proof that the property has passed a home inspection and termite, earthquake, or other inspections, depending on region. Your lender will order an appraisal of the property.

At this point, it's a good idea to tell your employer that the lender may be making inquiries about your job status, job security and length of employment. If you rent, let your landlord know too, in case the bank calls or writes. If you already have a mortgage, its holder may receive a request for a mortgage history rating too.

The Final Steps
Your lender is required by law to provide you with a good faith estimate within three business days of submitting your loan application. This document estimates the closing costs you will pay on purchase, and your monthly mortgage payments. The lender will also send you "A Home Buyer's Guide to Settlement Costs," a government publication.

Upon qualifying, you can assume that you have the mortgage. Congratulations!

What if I'm Turned Down?
If, after all that, your application is turned down, don't panic. Stay cool and ask your lender why. A sudden change in your credit rating, poor financial documentation, or having too small a down payment are common culprits.

Remember, your lender makes money by lending it. Your loan officer may be able to help you turn the situation around. Perhaps you can qualify for a smaller mortgage or can cobble together enough money to make a larger down payment. Maybe you can pay off more debt and then reapply.

If you are turned down, you probably will have to pay the lender's costs. These will include an application fee and credit report fee, among other items.

7

Making an Offer and Closing

You've seen the house you want. You are prequalified for a mortgage. You've checked out the property and the neighborhood, and your real estate agent agrees that this purchase makes economic sense.

Now it's time for you to make an offer and lock up the first of your acquisitions! In this chapter, we look at what your purchase offer should consist of and how to move through the closing procedures to occupancy of the property. And even though this chapter is more geared toward the first-time buyer, much of it applies to investment-grade properties, too. Financing choices might differ for investors, but settlement is usually quite similar between homebuyers and investors.

It's also helpful to remember that, with a pricey item like a building, the buyer and seller need to protect themselves. Rather than seeing the many procedures involved in buying a building as bothersome bureaucratic details, it makes better sense to view them as protective mechanisms. When put to use in your favor, any one of them can save you from making a mistake.

Making an Offer

You make a purchase offer for the property through your agent. If the seller accepts your offer, you both move toward closing. Ownership of the building actually changes hands at the closing (or "settlement") meeting.

In bygone times, when real estate markets were less active, there was plenty of time to mull over items such as price and terms when making a purchase offer for a property. That's all changed. In today's real estate market, you must make an offer on a desirable property as quickly as you can. I guarantee that, if you hesitate or dawdle over your bid, someone else will step in and take away your hard-found deal.

Your offer will resemble a contract and, once accepted and signed by both you and the seller, it becomes binding. It will probably include the following items:

- Price you want to pay
- Survey and legal description of the property you expect to receive
- Amount of your earnest money (a deposit to show you're serious
- Type of financing you are seeking
- Mortgage amount, with interest rate
- Expected closing date
- Expected occupancy date
- Furniture, fixtures, or other items to be included with the property
- Contingencies, which may include financing, repairs, home inspections, appraisal, environmental concerns, inspections, and ability of the seller to pro-

vide you with a clear title. (Clarify up front who pays for the title search. In some areas, this is negotiable.)

- Offer expiration date

Some of these items, such as furniture or contingencies, are usually negotiable. Should any of your contingencies not be met, be certain your offer stipulates a time frame to correct any shortcomings. If you encounter a deal-killer, make sure there's language in the offer that frees you from it without consequences. Your agent will know how to do this.

An Offer's Nuts and Bolts

Let's examine some of the components that make up an offer.

Down Payment

As we've seen previously, the down payment on a house, traditionally, was 20 percent of the total price. Mortgages available today permit you to pay as little as 3 to 5 percent of the purchase price. Your down payment requirement will vary according to your credit rating, income, the purchase price, and the kind of mortgage you select. You may not have to make a down payment at all.

For many mortgages, you have to save at least two months' of mortgage payments, called reserves. Most lenders will want to know where you found your down payment. Be careful volunteering this information; some lenders frown upon gifts from relatives or friends.

Earnest Money

To show good faith (that is, that you are ready, willing and able to buy) you generally include with your offer a cash deposit known as earnest money. The earnest money is deposited in an escrow account. If your deal goes through, the earnest money will go toward paying your closing costs. If you are responsible for a signed deal not being completed, you will probably lose your earnest money to the seller.

Closing Date

The sales contract should have an *estimated* closing or commitment date. After your loan application is accepted and you have signed the commitment letter, a closing date will be fixed. Your real estate agent, lender and closing agent may be the ones who fix this date. Be sure that the closing date occurs before your commitment letter expires, and while you still have an interest rate locked in.

The commitment letter gives the mortgage amount, terms of the loan, loan origination fee, discount points, annual percentage rate and monthly payments. The letter states a date by which you must accept and formally apply for the loan.

The closing agent should give you the closing date in writing, with the time and place of the closing meeting and a list of what records to bring with you.

Occupancy Date

Making a fixed occupancy date part of your purchase offer helps guarantee that you will take possession of the property in a timely manner after it has been bought. You should also include a provision that the seller has to pay you rent on the property if he or she has not vacated the premises by the occupancy date.

Contingencies

A contingency is a condition that must be fulfilled before a contract can be regarded as legally binding. Both the buyer and seller can have contingencies, and both parties often add that a "good faith effort" must be made to meet their conditions. Here are some common ones:

- A **loan contingency** means that you don't have to buy unless you qualify for a loan. Qualifying for a loan does not always mean that you will get one.

- An **offer** may be contingent on the property passing a building inspection or upon specified repairs being completed by the seller.

- With an **appraisal contingency**, if the building's appraised value does not reach a certain level, you get your earnest money back. The appraised value is its fair market value as estimated by a qualified appraiser. If this happens, it means you won't be able to get a mortgage, through no fault of yours. Sometimes, a seller will just drop the asking price to make the deal happen; others may let the deal go poof.

In reality, appraisals are highly subjective. Bank A's refusal to fund the deal doesn't mean Bank B won't—its appraiser might find more value in the property and grant you the mortgage. But treat any discrepancies in appraisals as expert, third-party advice about the deal you're making. Find out exactly what prompted the low appraisal, if you can, then proceed accordingly. Some appraisers are just more "buttoned down" than others are. But sometimes they're right too.

After You Make an Offer

Your real estate agent will convey your offer to the seller. A seller may accept or reject your offer, or make a counteroffer.

If the seller accepts, you move toward the closing or settlement. If the seller rejects your offer, or it is topped by a competing offer from another buyer, ask the agent if the bidding is still open. If it is, you must make up your mind—fast—about how much more to offer.

I assume you are bidding using *Bubble Proof* techniques, and are leaving enough wiggle room to move up in price if you must. I also assume you've already gotten more than enough of a prequalified mortgage commitment to cover any higher price situations. If not, then you may find yourself overextended if you have to see your lender about a new prequal that will enable you to make a higher bid. Never let yourself get boxed into a bidding war this way. As Kenny Rogers once sang, you got to know when to hold 'em, know when to fold 'em and walk away.

And, if the seller's counteroffer involves things other than price, be sure you completely understand everything involved and how the property's value may be affected.

You may wish to hire a real estate lawyer to review the sales contract before you sign it, especially if this is all new to you. In fact, some states require it. Your real estate agent may know a few attorneys, or you can find one yourself through your local bar association. Your lawyer's fees (ranging from $100 on up) are not part of the closing costs and must be paid by you independently.

If you wish, you can have your lawyer accompany you at the closing. Sometimes, investors will have their attorneys represent them at closings if they themselves are out of town.

Getting Ready for Closing

In the weeks before closing, you should be busy ensuring that you will have all the records, proofs and other items that the settlement documents require. Be sure your agent stays abreast of progress with title searches, lot surveys, termite inspections and other requirements.

Property Insurance

If you're buying with a mortgage, you will need to take out a property insurance policy on your new home. Why? Because, should something cause the destruction of a building that you own, you will probably still owe your lender the unpaid balance of the mortgage.

Policies cost several hundred dollars a year, and can be part of your regular mortgage payment. At closing, you'll probably need to prepay one full year's coverage.

There are two components to a good policy:

- **Casualty insurance** covers damage from fire, weather and most *but not all* other causes. You can select from four different kinds of casualty insurance:

  Actual cash value. Coverage is for the replacement value of the building, less depreciation.

  Replacement cost. Coverage is for the replacement value of the building with no deduction for depreciation. Therefore, it is set at a fixed maximum amount.

  Guaranteed replacement cost. Coverage is for the replacement value of the building with no deduction for depreciation and no fixed maximum amount.

  Extended replacement cost. Coverage is for the replacement value of the building plus a stated amount, generally 20 to 30 percent.

- **Liability insurance** covers injuries to visitors, theft, or damage to personal property.

If you're buying a rental property, your needs are somewhat different. You'll need a policy that covers the structure and potential liability stemming from tenant neglect. Check with your local insurers and get quotes.

Keeping Down Insurance Costs
You can keep down insurance costs in a number of ways.

- Insure only the building itself, not its contents or the ground beneath it.

- Install the anti-fire and anti-theft devices that your insurance company recommends.

- If you don't smoke, note this on the application form.

- A newer building should cost less to insure than an older one, especially a new building that has been constructed to resist fire and wind damage, and earthquakes.

- If you have car and other kinds of insurance, go to that company and ask for a preferred customer rate.

- If you're over a "certain age," ask for a discount.

- As with all insurance, the higher the deductible, the lower the cost.

Home Inspection

The older a building is, the likelier it is to have structural problems—though shoddy construction can cause even greater problems in more recent buildings. Hiring an independent, authorized home inspector to examine the building you want to buy may save you from unpleasant surprises later on.

These trained inspectors examine the place thoroughly, take pictures and issue a final report. They can find hidden defects in the roof, siding, or foundation—problems that can be hard for a non-professional to detect, but in time can develop into expensive repairs. They also can suggest ways to improve existing items prior to the sale (recommending caulking of windows, for example).

The inspector will also check the condition of the heating system; the presence or absence of insulating materials; and whether the electrical system is adequate. They can also check for the presence of hazardous materials, such as asbestos and lead paint.

Most sellers will not permit a private inspection until the paperwork is signed and the deal is going to closing. You can have a contingency item placed in your contract, however, that asks for a satisfactory report from an inspector, and ways to correct faults in the premises. *I encourage you to have this done,* even though you may pay several hundred dollars for the service. You can get more information from the American Society of Home Inspectors (ASHI) at www.ashi.org.

Survey

A survey is a map, or plot plan, depicting the property boundaries, improvements, easements, rights of way, encroachments and other physical features. Your lender will have a survey done, and you'll pay around $150 to $300 for it at settlement. If the property has been surveyed in the recent past, the surveyors may give you a reduced-price update. Be sure to ask about it.

Termite Inspection

The seller usually pays for a termite inspection, which is required in many areas before a property can be sold. The inspection certificate should state that the building is free of termite infestation and termite damage and carry some guarantee from the company that it will correct infestations it may have overlooked. Send the certificate to your lender before closing.

Title Search

A title search is required by most lenders to make sure the title to the property is clear of encumbrances. Encumbrances can include IRS liens and claims against the property for unpaid bills. The seller must settle all such encumbrances before or at the closing.

Final Walk-Through Inspection

Be sure you are allowed to make a last-minute walk-through inspection of the property before closing. On this inspection, you and your real estate agent can make sure that the seller has moved out of the property and left behind any lighting fixtures, window treatments or other items called for in the sale document. Check that the building's systems are intact, that everything works, the switches turn lights on and off, and that the faucets don't leak. If anything is awry, you can either delay the closing or insist on a so-called **mechanic's lien** at settlement. Such a lien will put some of the seller's proceeds in an escrow account to cover the costs of correcting the matter.

Going to Closing

The closing, or settlement, is the last step in purchasing a property. At the end of a successful closing, the property is yours. The seller, real estate agents and a closing agent will probably attend the closing with you. These sessions can occur at either agent's office; or a bank; or at the title company's office; or at your attorney's office.

Closing procedures differ from state to state, and may even vary from county to county. In some places, no closing meeting is held. Instead, an escrow agent sees that the papers are signed and funds change hands.

Closing Costs

Closing costs usually range from 3 to 6 percent of the loan amount. Although the seller pays some of these fees, the buyer pays most of them. At any rate, all these costs must be paid at closing in order for a sale to be finalized.

There are three kinds of costs: seller versus buyer costs, mortgage-related closing costs, and government-imposed closing costs. Let's look briefly at these costs.

Seller versus Buyer Closing Costs

Your contract will stipulate which costs the buyer will assume, and which the seller will assume. Occasionally, a sales contract might state that either the buyer or seller is paying *all* closing costs, but this is the exception, not the rule.

Mortgage-Related Closing Costs

These are closing costs that the mortgage maker will usually require the buyer to pay:

- **Loan origination fee.** This fee covers processing costs and is often quoted in points. A point equals 1 percent of the mortgage. Thus, a loan origination fee of one point for a $100,000 mortgage is $1,000.

- **Loan discount points.** Lenders charge these fees to lower the interest rate on a mortgage. For a 30-year mortgage, one discount point generally lowers the interest rate by 0.125 (one-eighth) percent.

- **Appraisal fee**

- **Credit report fee**

- **Assumption fee.** This fee is paid to the lender when the buyer takes over the payments on a loan previously made to the seller.

- **Prepaid interest**

- **Escrow accounts**

Government-Imposed Closing Costs

- **State and local taxes** are the most common forms of government-imposed closing costs. Property taxes are the ones most often negotiated between buyers and sellers. The resulting agreement is called an adjustment. A seller who has paid property taxes beyond the occupancy date may ask to be reimbursed by the buyer. If the seller owes property taxes from before the sale, the buyer may ask to have them deducted.

- A **recording fee** (a tax on recording the purchase documents into the government's records) and a **transfer tax** (a government fee on property transfers) are two other common closing costs.

You can estimate closing costs on purchases and sales of properties at the Freddie Mac Web site, www.freddiemac.com, by inserting dollar amounts for common settlement items.

Closing Documents
You should be given the following documents during, or shortly after, settlement:

- **Settlement statement.** This declares what the buyer and seller will each pay.

- **Promissory note.** This is your note to the lender detailing the terms of the mortgage and how you will pay it.

- **Affidavits.** These are sworn statements that you sign regarding various claims that you have made, such as your employment status and bank account amounts.

- **Deed.** This document transfers ownership of the property to you.

- **Title insurance document.**

Keep these documents in a safe place, along with copies of all documents you have signed and given to others. If anything goes wrong, you will need to refer to them. In addition, they can serve as records for possible tax deductions.

8

Reasons to Buy— from Every Angle

We've seen how renting can slowly, steadily drain away your ability to purchase your first home and keep you from investing in other wealth-building real estate in the coming years.

I realize that many of us start out as apartment dwellers. But I will never understand people who insist that they don't want to own property because it's too much of a headache. They become serial renters instead, tossing their cash to the wind month after month. That gives *me* a headache.

When people look seriously at their living arrangements, and do the rent-versus-buy math, the conclusion is plain. But sometimes, other factors tug at them. How many times folks have told me, "My apartment is convenient to where I work" or "We're in no hurry to buy a house, because we aren't starting a family for a while." When I finally show them, with numbers, how far ahead they'll be by buying now, I see the lights go on. At last, they begin asking themselves questions they had brushed off before.

Why Your Landlord Loves You

If you're still renting, you should understand the many ways you're enriching your landlord. You see, renting isn't just a matter of writing a check to the landlord every month.

You might pay $1,000 a month in rent, which amounts to $12,000 a year, to your landlord. And while you're looking at your rent payment in a very short-term context (once a month), your landlord is looking at you as a long-term investment! Let's do the math: With an average annual rent increase of just 3 percent, in 10 years you'll have paid the landlord more than $137,500.

But wait, there's more. Each year the landlord is increasing the equity in the building you're renting, as he or she pays off the mortgage—using your rent payments.

The landlord also realizes substantial deductions on interest and property taxes, so he or she enjoys annual tax savings. Most renters I know can only file a 1040EZ tax return because they don't have the deductions a mortgage provides.

And the value of the building where you rent keeps rising in most years. It's in a good location, convenient to shopping and transit lines. At the end of 10 years, it may be worth twice what it is today. Thanks to you and your fellow tenants, the landlord will benefit from all that appreciation. After all, he or she owns the building.

Still wondering why the landlord sees a walking paycheck every time you pass by?

Co-Op, Condo or Townhouse?

Most people enter the real estate market by purchasing a single-family house, but this is not the only way to do it. You can purchase a co-op apartment unit, a condominium or a townhouse. It's really a question of what will work best for you. Let's look at these purchasing alternatives.

Co-Op Apartment

Sometimes, the question of what to buy turns on the down payment more so than the mortgage, locality or buyers' needs. If that's the case, buying a co-op apartment might make the most sense. Co-ops are groups of apartments; each apartment is individually owner-occupied. However, the common walls, grounds and other shared amenities are shared, so their upkeep is paid for by every owner through dues.

Advantages: Down payments and closing costs are usually much less than for houses. Because you take out a mortgage, you build equity over time, and reap beneficial tax deductions every year. And as an owner, you'll maintain an apartment lifestyle without the landlord.

Disadvantages: You may have to shop a while before you find a lender that understands co-op financing, since they're a relatively new kind of ownership. If you decide to buy an apartment, you'll pay a monthly maintenance fee. Review the co-op's regulations thoroughly beforehand.

Condominium

Although I firmly believe that first-time buyers should look at purchasing a house first, that's just not a practical alternative for some people. Luckily, condominium living offers many of the same financial and tax advantages as owning a house, albeit on a smaller scale—and there's no grass to cut.

Condos are a hybrid of sorts: They're like a fancy apartment that you own instead of rent. They have the advantage of affordable living in great locations: close to cities or resort areas, and nearer to public transit and attractions.

Condominiums demand careful scrutiny, however. You'll need to decide whether you want to pay monthly fees to enjoy the pool, gym, sauna and lovely landscaping. And it's important to find out if the building's management and residents are playing nicely together, or bickering over costs and maintenance. Find out if the association fees have stayed fairly constant or if they've been going up a lot each year. Lastly, ask to see a full copy of the condo's rules, bylaws and covenants and read them cover to cover. If you find them onerous, you should look elsewhere.

That said, most newer condos are good investments and good places to live. (Avoid anything built in the 1980s condo boom; many were poorly constructed.) They can be an affordable way to enjoy a city lifestyle or have a home of your own without the upkeep hassles.

As far as the purchasing process goes, buying a condo is quite like buying a home. You need to determine whether the condo market is stable and if values are appreciating. You'll also need to review the plethora of mortgages to be sure you choose the right one. Most of the time, you can secure a mortgage with a down payment under 20 percent.

Advantages: Convenience, location and affordability.

Disadvantages: Condos should be considered a specialty type of homeownership, so the resale market is narrower. Previewing the building, neighborhood, condo association rules and management entity is crucial to avoid buying a lemon.

Townhouse

Townhouses go by several names: attached house; semidetached house; row home or even brownstone. There are subtle differences among them, mostly having to do with how many walls two townhouses might share.

More important are the questions of lifestyle and appreciation of your townhouse over time, and in both cases the news is good.

Unlike condos or co-ops, townhouses are much more house-like. Although attached to each other, they can be spacious, with several floors, a garage and even a small fenced-in back yard. Even better, because they are constructed side by side, they share a common foundation and other construction-related items. Therefore, townhouses will cost somewhat less than a detached house of similar proportions.

Again, before buying, thoroughly investigate the surrounding area, to make sure the market will support your investment. And keep in mind that, in a townhouse with shared walls, you live as close to your neighbors as humanly possible without moving into their unit! So make certain the building has very good sound abatement and that there's enough privacy to suit you.

Advantages: Townhouses make a sound investment choice when the price of a detached house is out of reach. You own your townhouse. This segment of the real estate business has been growing in popularity, so demand is increasing.

Most townhouse communities include pools and community centers that need maintenance, so expect to pay an association fee on top of your mortgage.

Disadvantages: Townhouses can feel boxy. Be sure yours has a spacious feel with plenty of windows, since sunlight can be at a premium. Repairs to a roof or facade might require every owner in a block of townhouses to participate. See if any restrictive covenants are in place that regulate paint schemes, yard decorations and other common issues.

But I Like Living in My Apartment!

If you have a happy living arrangement or bargain rent (if, say, your parents own your unit), you don't have to give it up in order to invest in real estate. I always advise renters who insist on living where they are to purchase a nonowner-occupied property.

If you choose this option, start by buying a house to rent, or even better, a duplex. Remember, with a duplex you won't be left high and dry if one of your tenants moves out. Your other tenant will still produce rent to help tide you over while you find new renters.

After gaining experience for a few years in small-scale rentals, I tell clients to step up to a multi-unit apartment house, like the one they live in. They may even decide to become full-time property managers and investors at that point, and I'll have accomplished my mission—getting them involved in real estate—via an alternate route.

How to Spot an All-Star Real Estate Agent

Let's say you're ready to buy your first house. You realize that you need a good real estate agent to make it happen. But how can you tell if an agent is an all-star?

- As someone who's bought and sold houses many times, and helped hundreds of other folks do the same, I know the ropes about real estate. So here are a few pointers on how to spot the telltale signs of a good agent:

- The agent is not a Johnny-come-lately to the business. Instead, the agent has years of experience.

- The agent is a full-time agent, not a part-timer or weekend warrior.

- The agent is upfront about the market and is proud to share his or her sales numbers over the past 12 months.

- When asked for recommendations from former clients, the agent has a sheaf of references and encourages you to call any of them.

- The agent does a lot of listening, and takes occasional notes, instead of launching into a sales pitch right away.

- The agent has detailed information about the best areas for singles, retirees, families, or career-minded couples.

- The agent is thorough about mortgage programs, schools, neighborhood features and other points of interest.

- The agent realizes that first-timers are often uncertain about how to proceed, and will patiently explain the options that make the most sense, and how to proceed.

Here's another suggestion: After seeing homes with your agent, drive through the neighborhoods you like by yourself. Go at different times of the day and night, on weekdays and weekends. It's surprising how each will differ from the other as well as from the neighborhood in which you're living now. In some, you may see lots of playgrounds, schools and churches, but very few bars and upscale restaurants. In others, the opposite may be true and the nightlife may·be the attraction.

You should also check the U.S. Department of Housing and Urban Development Web site (www.hud.gov) and review HUD's Neighborhood and Location Checklist to size up various locations. See if they have the features you want in a community. The checklist is a very thorough and thought-provoking tool to help you make the most of your house hunting.

What Kind of House and How Much?

If you're clueless about what houses cost, an hour or two with your real estate agent will give you a quick education.

After reviewing your mortgage prequalification letter, a good agent will prepare computerized lists for you. The lists show the kinds of houses that sold over the past few months, and where the sales occurred. But remember—it's not always about price. The question to ask your agent is whether those areas have seen significant increases in values over the past few years. If so, has the growth in prices topped out or has it just begun?

You might also be surprised at how certain kinds of houses seem to command certain prices. If you're house hunting with a spouse or partner, you may find that you have wildly different expectations of what your home should be. Don't wait until you're out with your agent before you at least discuss, generally, what kind of house you'd like. Two-story or ranch? Split level? Colonial, modern or traditional style? By churning through some of these topics beforehand, you'll have a much clearer idea of what you really want and the agent will have a much better idea of what to show.

Keep in mind, too, that in most cases, a higher-priced home tends to offer you more wealth-building potential over time than small ones do. That's because of two things. First, a higher-priced house will appreciate more in value. For example, if houses rose in value by 5 percent in a year, a $200,000 house would be worth $10,000 more while a $300,000 house would increase by $15,000 in value. Second, you would get greater tax write-offs and deductions from the higher-priced home.

That said, don't be too aggressive. If you plan to start a family soon, you may be better suited in a smaller, more manageable mortgage.

You'll also discover that home prices are influenced by where they're located too. Obviously, shady, quiet streets are ideal for many buyers. But commuters might need a place within walking distance to the railway station. Others might want a small town, or a rural setting. The factors that can make a difference in where you buy are plentiful:

- Price range
- Style of the home
- Older, recent or brand new home
- Condition of the home (fixer-upper, minor repairs or mint)
- In town or no
- Near shopping
- Schools (some buyers don't want to be near schools)
- Public transportation

- Yard size
- Fenced or not (for kids, pets, pool)
- View
- Near recreation (golf course, tennis courts, etc.)
- Gated or open access

Talking the Talk:
Speak Like a Real Estate Agent

Almost every business and profession has its own terminology and jargon. People who can talk the talk get treated with respect as insiders.

To invest in real estate you don't have to know weird-sounding slang or Latin phrases, but you do have to understand the meaning of such terms as *escrow fee* and *origination fee*. The reason you need to understand them is that you will be signing agreements in which these terms frequently appear.

My number one rule regarding any agreement, not just in real estate, is never sign one you do not fully understand.

Looking at the dotted line of a property contract is no time to start learning the meaning of terms. Knowing the meaning of jargon and terms allows you to ask questions, pursue explanations and include some additional protective items in the agreement.

Ask lots of questions about contracts and contingencies beforehand. I've included a glossary of terms at the end of *Bubble Proof* to assist you. Your agent should have a publication for you that deciphers common terminology. The Internet, of course, has reams of useful definitions and examples. And get your money's worth from your attorney, if you decide to retain one to handle your transactions. After all, lawyers wrote most of the clauses in contracts to begin with!

PART III

MAXIMIZING
THE OWNERSHIP
OPPORTUNITY

9

Investing in
Multi-Unit Properties

While a single-family home is most people's first preference, the economics of owning multi-unit properties might make you think again, especially if you are just starting out.

There are two strategies to think about here. In the first strategy, you buy your first house, and then use it as leverage to acquire a second, multi-unit building. In the second, you use your money to buy a multi-unit building, live in one of the units and rent the rest.

A multi-unit building, for this chapter, means a structure that has two, three or four units. Thus, a duplex house, which contains two living units sharing a middle dividing wall but having separate entrances, is a multi-unit building. Sometimes, the two units are side by side. Other times, they consist of a two-story building in which the renting family occupies the upper floor and the owning family the lower floor.

Three- and four-unit buildings come in all shapes and sizes, and can be found above storefronts as well as in stand-alone structures. In many parts of America, three-bedroom units are termed "triplexes."

Doubling Up for Savings

In a well-planned multi-family lease, the renting families' monthly rents cover the owning family's monthly mortgage payments, annual property taxes and maintenance costs of the building. In other words, the owning family lives in its unit for a greatly reduced amount, and often at no cost whatsoever.

This approach sidesteps one of the biggest fears of first-time, single-family homebuyers—that some disaster will cause them to lose the property because they can't meet the payments. However, that's only one of several benefits that the owners enjoy. As I've discussed already, the owners acquire increasing equity in the building as the mortgage is paid off by the renting family. The owners gain wealth as the building's value appreciates over the years. And each tax season, the owners receive hefty deductions on their returns.

You can use a duplex house as a passport into a neighborhood in which you could not afford to live in a single-family home. Alternatively, if you can get a mortgage to seal the deal, a three- or four-unit building in a more affluent neighborhood is to your advantage too. These situations command higher rents, and bring a better clientele that is apt to stay—and pay—for a longer period of time.

Multi-Unit Apartment Buildings

Perhaps the most rewarding real estate opportunity for most investors is to buy an apartment building with no more than four units. From my experience working with buyers, four seems to be the magic number that generally keeps a building from becoming subject to complex city regulations.

Just as I urged you to steep yourself in your local rental laws, you ought to check into zoning and building regulations too. They are highly variable. Most of the time, they are reasonable; but in some jurisdictions they can be downright onerous. Real estate agents with experience in apartment-house restrictions can give you good advice on this.

As long as you don't uncover a deal-killing problem with the building, neighborhood or local regulations, there's no reason to shy away from buying, and moving into, a multi-unit apartment building. For example, most people who consider buying such a building worry about how they would collect the rents. In my experience, this has seldom been a problem. The vast majority of tenants simply drop off their rent every month. And if they don't, it's almost always because they simply forgot to do so. A friendly knock on their door or phone call remedies the situation without further ado.

You may also wonder about upkeep. Usually, the units are renovated between tenants, so most "big" problems are corrected at these times. After tenants move in, a faucet starts dripping or an appliance needs attention. Many investors enjoy making repairs themselves for their tenants. For those tasks you can't get to, or are beyond your abilities, you have a handyman on call. He or she can solve these various problems when you can't. One other option is to hire a professional property management company; we'll discuss this in further detail later on.

Finding Worthwhile Tenants

Screening for applicants who are economically stable, respectful of your property and who conduct themselves civilly is likely to be your biggest chore. But it needn't be so difficult that you look forward to scraping the paint off the exterior because it would be a relief!

Whether you're living in one of the units or off-premises, you need renters that you can get along with, and who can get along with others. Any time you screen applicants, make sure your spouse or partner is part of the screening process, and listen carefully to their point of view. After all, there will be times that they'll have contact with the renters. If for any reason an applicant rubs either of you the wrong way, move on!

Trust your instincts but go with facts. You can obtain reliable credit information on applicants in several ways. Most of these reports will include, for a fee, additional information on civil suits and court actions. Since these are public records, you can obtain them all legally. Don't enter any arrangement in which the tenants have previously been to court—as either plaintiffs or defendants—with their landlord.

Your applicants expect to give you personal information as part of the renting process. But don't stop there. Call where they say they work and make sure they are employed. Call previous landlords and other references. Never rent to anyone without first checking his or her background. These days, you just never know.

You'll also need to understand the laws protecting landlords and tenants. They can vary widely by state, county and city. I've heard horror stories about tenants who move in and then just stop paying rent. Yet they are so good at manipulating the law and crying foul at every opportunity that landlords must fight for months to get rid of them. Even when the law seems unquestionably to be in their favor, the courts can take forever before ruling. Sometimes, judgments go against the landlord and must be appealed before justice is served. Then, when the tenants finally are evicted, they leave the unit looking like a bomb site. And in a surprising number of these incidents, the landlords failed to check out the tenants beforehand.

I also think people should be wary of renting to family and friends. I admit it can have good points—you know the tenants like the back of your hand, and probably will never have a serious problem with their behavior. Yet, the biggest disadvantage may be that same familiarity. Family or friends may think it's okay to pay the rent late on occasion, or adopt a puppy without asking you first.

By making smart decisions ahead of time and following the commandment of renting—Thou Shalt Check Tenants' Background Thoroughly Before Giving Them a Key—you will find your tenants are good people…reliable, friendly and good caretakers. They'll be the kind of tenants you'll really hate to see leave when they finally buy a place of their own.

Financing Multi-Unit Purchases

Multi-unit mortgages vary somewhat from their plain vanilla, single-family cousins. One vital fact, though, is that lenders tend to have more confidence in buildings that are owner occupied. And they expect to see not just income projections, but realistic expense projections too. Be prepared to discuss who will be cutting the grass, shoveling the snow and washing the outside of the windows too.

It's also important to establish clearly that your investment will produce positive cash flow. There are simple ways to do this. One of the best ways is to ask the seller for his or her Schedule E, which is a tax document showing rents, upkeep expenses and net gain or loss for the year. (Remember, net loss doesn't mean you're not making money. Most landlords will show losses after deductions, depreciation and write-offs.)

You can also check the classifieds, and perhaps even the Internet, to compare your prospective purchase to other, similar multi-unit rentals. If you know that another landlord is getting $1,500 a month for two-bedroom, one-bathroom units in the same vicinity, you can peg your projected number to those figures.

Don't make the mistake of calculating your rental income by assuming you'll have a full house all year. Instead, calculate the building's rent potential at 85 percent instead of 100. Nine times out of ten, you'll have at least one tenant moving out and you'll need time to spruce up the unit and find a suitable new renter. Set aside another 10 percent of your monthly gross income for sudden repairs and emergencies.

In case of vacancies, time is definitely money! Get the place fixed up. Have the carpets shampooed, the walls painted and the kitchen and bath looking good, so you can begin showing it as soon as possible. And start looking for new tenants while you're doing that, not afterward. Prospective tenants don't mind seeing a work in progress—as long as the apartment doesn't look beat up.

Finally, get estimates on insurance as well as copies of the previous owner's sewer, water, cable TV, electricity and heating bills before you make your offer. Although you may be able to allocate most of these expenses to the tenants, some of them (water, heat, sewer) remain your responsibility by law.

In some cities, you may be offered 100 percent financing with no down payment to buy a multi-unit dwelling. The catch is that the building must be in a particular low-income neighborhood and must be below a certain price. You are not getting something for nothing. Essentially, you are being offered a building worth up to perhaps $400,000 in exchange for your management skills, optimism and belief in the community. You will earn ownership of the building in other ways than exchanging money for it. For someone with the energy, perseverance and courage, this can be a life-changing opportunity.

10

Fixer-Uppers

Every opportunity you uncover will have its own advantages and drawbacks. After you've successfully bought, sold and invested, you'll see a pattern emerge. You'll discover that the opportunities in which you are the most successful are the ones whose plusses and minuses you handle most adroitly. In many ways, it's all about you!

This comes back to knowing your own strengths and weaknesses. As individuals, we have inherent strengths that make us more effective in some kinds of real estate opportunities than others. The truly skilled investors, of course, look for chances in which both innate and learned skills guide them to another successful purchase or sale.

One of the most important lessons of the *Bubble Proof* method is to stop seeing real estate *as it is* and to start seeing it in terms of *what it can be*. Nowhere does this tactic come more into play than with "fixer-upper" homes. These are diamonds in the rough in every sense. They may look, and even sometimes smell, bad—but the eagle-eyed first-time buyer or investor sees nothing but beauty. Ordinary, uninformed house hunters see an ugly, unlovable dump.

And that's good! If everyone were able to see how great a property might look and how gratifying the return-on-investment in these places can be, then you and I might be a lot poorer! But most buyers either can't see the hidden values in a fixer, or they couldn't be bothered with refurbishing it. "Too much work," they'll say with a sniff. To which I say, "Too bad for you."

It Is What It Is

Let's nail down the definition of fixer-upper first. Fixers are homes that have been neglected by their owners, but haven't been subjected to the misery of foreclosure or abandonment. Every neighborhood has certain houses that look spectacular while others look as if the owners have been away on a five-year cruise. They become, for lack of a more diplomatic term, eyesores. But believe me, when they go up for sale, they can be gold mines for first-time buyers and investors.

Fixer-uppers are undervalued for their neighborhood because the owner has let the property slip. As such, they are less expensive and are a great way for you to get into a neighborhood that you would be priced out of otherwise. As long as the property doesn't have a deal-killing structural defect, and you're ready to endure some construction noise and a little dirt, you should pursue fixer-uppers aggressively.

Please note the distinction between "fixers" and "foreclosures." You may be surprised to find that I don't include foreclosures among my recommended real estate opportunities. The truth is that I have too many qualms about them to recommend them as a wealth-building strategy.

I realize I'm swimming against the popular tide here. It's true that some investors-turned-pitchmen have made money—sometimes, lots of it—going to foreclosure auctions and flipping houses. But I think a few words of caution here are essential.

While it's true that properties seized by creditors for nonpayment are often auctioned off at rock bottom prices, there are often good reasons for this. Foreclosures or abandonments often have "dirty" titles, with tax or other liens against them, as well as other legal problems. In fact, properties are sometimes abandoned by their owners because of their intractable legal problems. Even if you perform due diligence that would make a real estate attorney proud, some property titles can never be made right in time for you to cash in.

Besides this, many foreclosure sales are for cash. Financing is hard to get for foreclosures, and you may find yourself bidding against professionals with inside knowledge and connections.

On a personal note, I also don't like foreclosures because of the feeling that I'd be benefiting from someone else's misfortune. In every foreclosure, someone lost a home...and usually the circumstances were heart-rending. I often find these homes to be sad and forlorn, no matter how bright and cheerful you try to make them.

To my dismay, some of my clients insist on pursuing foreclosed homes as a wealth-building strategy, in spite of my yellow flag waving. So, I'll be realistic, and admit that some of you readers might do so too. Just remember: If you are able to purchase a foreclosed property at a bargain price, don't forget that everything in that house will become yours, including any baggage that comes with it. Enough said.

Sizing Up a Fixer-Upper

One day I came upon a brick, one-story rancher in a good section of Austin, where I was living at the time. The house was in desperate need of some work. From curbside, the couple I was with took one look and blanched. We drove away, but afterwards, I returned to the house and asked the elderly owners if I could look inside. They agreed, as Texans are inclined to do!

The house needed a new roof. Some of the upstairs windows were so old they didn't close properly. Most of the bedroom doors hung crooked. The paint was dirty inside, the trim was peeling outside, and vines climbed up its exterior walls. But none of that mattered to me. It had hardwood floors, a fireplace, a big (albeit neglected) shady yard and fixtures that were all in working order.

As I had suspected earlier in the day, it was a perfect fixer-upper.

Knowing I was going to make an offer on the house, I walked through the long grass, viewing the house from all angles. I did some quick math. Homes in good shape sold for around $170,000 in the neighborhood. I estimated it would cost $12,000 in materials and labor to bring this house into the same condition of other houses in the area. I also estimated that my closing costs on a mortgage would come in at no more than $8,000.

I decided that, if I bought this property for a good price, fixed it and then sold in a few years, neighborhood values would be nearing $185,000 if not more. I couldn't see a downside. The building's structural condition was sound (later confirmed by the inspector I hired) but with a little TLC, it would pay off handsomely.

So, I pounced. My first offer was for $125,000 even though the house listed for $155,000.

The owners countered only once—to $130,000—and the deal was done. Three years later, I sold it for $189,900! And since my closing only amounted to $6,000 and repairs were only $10,500, my final "net" was $43,400 on a $16,500 investment.

*   *   *

As is usually the case with these kinds of homes, the house I bought looked much worse than it actually was. In real estate, looks are often deceiving. Many would-be owners are saddled with the misconception that fixers are a lot of grief and no profit.

People who deal in fixer-uppers have to know: (1) how much certain alterations will raise a building's value; and (2) how much those particular alterations are going to cost. You have to know a neighborhood well, and understand what the people expect from a typical home.

If you expect to sell your fixer in the near future, ask yourself who will live there after you, what they are willing to pay for. As an example, in Austin, you're expected to have central air in your home. Window units are considered low income, and will detract from the value of a moderately priced home. But is this also true in, say, North Dakota, where I was born? Not at all. So you see, different neighborhoods have different expectation levels. The trick is to make your fixer house as much like the nice homes on the block as you can—without making the common mistake of underestimating your costs.

Sometimes, fixer-uppers have zero built-in upside. They may be located in an area that's on the way down, where most of the houses are being neglected.

Not all fixer-uppers show enough margin of profit, either, for them to be worthwhile purchases or investments. They may be situated in a town where growth, though it occurs, is slower than you desire. A good rule of thumb is to come away with at least $10,000 more than you put into a fixer, or else, what is the point? They take work, and let's face it: We don't have the time to waste on investments with puny returns.

But, if you're careful and remember your bubble-proofing techniques, fixer-uppers can be lucrative. Clever, cost-effective cosmetic repairs are sometimes all it takes to transform their appearance from "frog" to "prince" (or "princess," depending upon who's doing the buying).

Fannie Mae and Freddie Mac offer fixer-upper loans for owners (but not investors), as do several government programs. The HUD Section 203(k) loan program is the most widely used. This program finances major rehabilitation work on buildings more than a year old with one to four units. Condos are ineligible for these loans. The 203(k) loan can be used for renovations only, or it can be combined with a purchasing loan to buy and work on a fixer-upper.

I Repeat: Keep Your Costs Down

In Chapter 3, I warned about the dangers of self-deception when doing rehab work, either to your home or to your investment properties. We tend to want to rehab our properties to our own tastes, and this usually leads us to bust our budgets.

Earlier in this chapter, I mentioned the dust and noise involved with fixer-uppers. However, I still think that carefully controlled rehabbing helps to make fixers such a big real estate investment opportunity.

If you're a first-time buyer, you don't have to borrow as much money to buy a fixer. You can move into the house and learn to live "around" the work in progress. You can do much of the work yourself, if you choose. That way, you control the timing and expenditures. There is an old rule that I have found useful: Carefully estimate your costs in detail and then multiply the amount by two. It is amazing how things cost almost exactly twice what you first thought they might.

The advantages of rehabbing a fixer-upper very often trump the reasons to buy a house in "move-in" condition—as long as you don't get carried away buying supplies at the home center!

11

Home, Sweet
Second Home

Sooner or later, all real estate investors will face the question of buying or building a second home for themselves.

The second home market has existed for many years. But it really came to the forefront in the late 1990s and the earliest years of this century, as more and more affluent Americans decided to obtain an idyllic getaway spot that they could enjoy for vacations and weekend retreats. And, naturally, we all have to retire someday, so why not in a place we love?

"Hot markets" for second homes and condos come and go. I don't recommend trying to chase them as investment opportunities. Today's hot market for golf-course homes inevitably gives way to tomorrow's "hot" seaside condo buildings. So, before buying in an area where real estate is booming, stand back and understand *why* one place is hotter than somewhere else.

Much of what drives second-home markets is old-fashioned personal taste. We all have our own notions about relaxation, peace and quiet, amusement and living the good life. If you want to live by the seashore, then Las Vegas or Orlando are not for you. But if Las Vegas appeals to you as a vacation spot, the serenity of the mountains would never appeal to you.

Hot markets offer liquidity, meaning that it is easy to resell on good terms anytime you want. But the fact is, you don't need to buy into a hot market to make a worthwhile investment in a second home. Buying in a less active place may require holding onto a property longer than you would like, but in the end your profit may be greater because the purchase price was lower. In some situations, even buying into an as-yet undeveloped resort area can be an excellent investment too.

While it is always appropriate to think location, location, location, much depends on your expectations. My general rule is to buy in places where people want to live. Finding these places is not difficult and often they aren't anywhere near "hot" markets.

Remember: When a certain location catches fire, speculation is often at work. That's tantamount to gambling from my perspective, and it has no place in the *Bubble Proof* approach. I might buy in a neighborhood that is rundown but improving, but I don't bet on its gentrification to suddenly speed up. Neighborhoods tend to take their time. Here again, expectations become very important.

Condos for Real People (Like Us)

As we've already discussed, a condominium is a building in which the units are separately owned, but with joint ownership of shared building areas and the grounds. The units themselves are usually called condos. A board runs the building on a day-to-day basis and maintains only control over the unit owners.

In some Eastern and Midwestern cities, you can buy a cooperative apartment. Members occupy a specific apartment and hold shares in the cooperative that owns or controls the apartment building. The co-op board has a veto on buyers and other matters, which sometimes results in power falling into the hands of a few individuals. From an investor's point of view, condo ownership provides far more freedom to buy or sell as you please than a co-op.

While single-family homes remain, by far, the most popular real estate investment, condos are fast gaining widespread acceptance. About one in every ten homes sold today is a condo. Two separate population groups invest in condos heavily. Empty nesters—couples whose children have grown and left home—are one group. They sell their relatively large homes at high prices and move to smaller condos. The other group is composed of young couples and singles who, as first-time homebuyers, choose a condo over a single-family home. To me, these two diverse and growing groups would seem to insure a lively market in condos for some years to come.

Almost a million condos are sold each year, and their yearly price appreciation often rivals that of single-family homes. Because condos need much less hands-on attention than houses, they are attractive investments to owners who do not occupy them or who live elsewhere. In buying a condo as a rental property, however, do not expect that the rent will always cover the monthly mortgage payment and maintenance fee, as you often can with a house. With a condo, your payoff comes with the increase in its value when you sell.

Before buying a condo at a resort, make sure there are no restrictions on renting, should you wish to do so. Be prepared to pay a relatively high purchase price for a property at a popular resort. There are few bargain-priced items at well-known venues. Instead, you have to decide whether prices will continue to climb and make your purchase worthwhile.

As you have most likely read in the news, some people trade their condos before they even physically exist. One story I read concerned a speculator in Miami who got a call from his real estate agent, stopped by her office and put down a deposit on two condos, without even seeing the floor plans. Not long afterward, he heard from her again. This time she had a buyer for his two condos at a price that gave him a big profit. The builder hadn't even broken ground yet to start construction of the building.

Notice that I said *speculator* rather than investor. Speculators put large sums into what are very often high-risk ventures. To move at the speed required in such deals, they need open lines of credit from banks. In addition to buying and closing costs and agent commissions, they face a big tax bite on selling. Their federal short-term capital gains taxes can be up to 35 percent if they sell within a year of purchasing, and 15 percent if they wait a year. No doubt, there are often large overnight profits, but I only hope these wheelers and dealers in real estate know exactly what they are doing. If they don't, they may end up flipping burgers instead of condos.

Be very careful if you buy into an unbuilt condominium. Developers have clamped down on buyers who "flip" their purchase for a windfall, which means straight shooters have to sign onerous, and maybe unbreakable, purchase commitments. Additionally, you should have a better-than-average grasp of the locality you are buying in, to protect yourself from making a major blunder. If your main source of knowledge is a glossy pamphlet with pretty photos, you have not done your homework.

Here's an example of how the process of buying a new condo is supposed to work, without the speculators. On Alabama's Gulf Coast, developers who wish to construct a condominium advertise to sell them for $500,000 to $1 million. The developers must "presell" at least 60 percent of the units before getting construction financing.

The developer lets each buyer reserve one or more units with a small cash down payment. The buyer then has up to 60 days to obtain a letter of credit from a bank to cover the down payment of 20 percent of the purchase price. The reservation becomes a sale on the buyer's delivery of the letter of credit to the seller, and the buyer's cash deposit is returned.

Construction time is estimated at two years, and the bank charges the buyer a fee of 1 to 3 percent of the letter of credit value per year. In effect, the investor buys without tying up any cash.

On the other hand, brokers in New York City recommend that anyone wanting to sell a condo at a choice Manhattan location should consult with adjoining neighbors and those on floors immediately above and below. Condos that share a common wall, or whose ceilings and floors join, are being packaged as duplexes or triplexes—and selling together for much more per unit than they would singly.

Vacation and Second Homes

In a typical year, Americans buy more than half a million second homes. Four out of five are vacation homes; the others are single-family rental properties.

Single-family homes are the most popular kind of second home, although condos are gaining in popularity. And even though second homes tend to be smaller, they can be just as expensive as homes in your primary neighborhood—if they're in popular places.

Rather than placing big bets at established resorts, I advise many real estate investors to buy at much lower prices in places that are near, but not in, vacation or getaway destinations. These places are pleasant and convenient, and usually just a short distance inland from the sea, or not quite on the slopes of picturesque mountains. Nonetheless, they are easy to reach and enjoyable in themselves.

If you are the kind of person who does not have to be at the center of things, you may find such places highly appealing. Certainly, heavy traffic and crowded resorts make these almost anonymous towns appealing for increasing numbers of investors. It is worth noting that computers and home offices now enable people to live and work full time in pleasant towns that are convenient to major resorts and big cities, but somewhat off the beaten track.

Should You Buy?

Should you buy a vacation home? Certainly you should, if you can afford one and enjoy recreation. However, I suggest that you consider the financial aspects before you start looking at properties.

What can you afford as a down payment? Most lenders will expect a down payment of 20 percent. You are unlikely to get as favorable an interest rate as you would for a primary home, because the default rate on vacation homes is higher. Your mortgage payments will amount to at least $1,000 a month. Since the main point of a vacation home is to reduce your stress level, you must be sure that you can manage the down payment and mortgage payments in spite of the fact that your second home won't throw off any cash (unless you rent it, of course).

On the positive side, you can buy a vacation home and gain benefits similar to those of your primary home, including:

- **Price appreciation.** Buy a second home and watch the value of your property increase.

- **Amortization.** As you pay off your mortgage, your equity in the property increases.

- **Tax benefits.** Unless you rent out your second home for more than 14 days a year, it has all the tax deductions of your primary residence.

- **Emotional and health benefits.** A vacation home can operate as a safety valve for the pressures of daily life. A change of scenery helps keep things in perspective. You are also likely to take in more exercise and breathe fresher air.

- **Vacation expenses saved.** Hotel, resort and restaurant prices alone make vacation home ownership a recreational bargain.

- **Capital gains exclusion.** On selling your second home, you can qualify for a capital gains exclusion of $500,000 on a joint return ($250,000 on a single), if you have used the property as your principal residence for at least two of the five years before selling. (When selling a rental property, seek professional advice on tax deferment through purchasing another property under a Section 1031 exchange.)

- **Future retirement home.** You can sell your primary residence, with a capital gains exclusion of $500,000 on a joint return, and retire to the vacation home you bought at a moderate price.

Where to Buy

With a vacation home, you should follow your own interests in selecting its location. If you are an avid skier, you know which resort towns are already overcrowded and overpriced. You're not going to buy in one of those.

You probably know or have heard about accessible towns near great skiing country that are only now being developed. Those are the kinds of places in which to buy, but only after you have checked firsthand on their potential. Don't rely on the judgment of friends; investigate for yourself. Find out why the area has not been developed before now. Be sure you know the real story.

Does the vacation area you are considering have a single season or do people come there in other seasons? For example, a ski resort in winter may be a fishing or hiking resort in summer, and a hunting resort in fall.

Ask lots of questions:

- Is the resort popular with only certain kinds of people?
- Is the terrain so rugged that only young, athletic people come?
- Do bars and clubs keep families away?
- In time, could this be your retirement home?

Vacation Home versus Rental Property

When you rent your second home for less than 14 days a year, you do not have to pay federal income tax on any rental income, but of course you can't deduct any expenses involved in renting, either. You can still deduct property taxes and mortgage interest on your vacation home from your taxes, just as you can with your primary home.

When you rent for 14 days or more a year, your second home is regarded by the Internal Revenue Service as a rental property for tax purposes. This means that your rental income is taxable. However, your rental expenses (maintenance, advertising for tenants) are deductible, as are depreciation, property taxes and mortgage interest.

Using a Management Company

If you rent your second home and it is some distance from where you live, your first inclination might be to hire a professional property management company to correct problems and collect rent.

At a resort, finding a steady flow of short-term tenants is the most important service such a company can provide. Your property should be rented full time during the high season, and for as much time as possible in the off-season. If you retain a management firm, make certain that your property is included in its online multiple listings and in tourist magazine ads. It's also their job to screen prospective tenants, collect deposits, and provide all necessary services, including cleaning, plumbing and electrical work. Finally, they should forward a complete account of all transactions and funds due to you.

But be advised: Finding a company to perform these functions and maintain the property in rentable condition can cost up to 50 percent of the rental income. If the rent is high and the property has a good occupancy record, paying a big commission to a competent management company might make sense. However, before purchasing such a property, do the math. You don't want the management company to be the only party to do well from this arrangement. You can get sound advice on management firms from a local, experienced buyer's agent. At any rate, renting a single-family rental property with a steady tenant is a much simpler undertaking and should cost you about 7 percent of the rental income. Finding and screening a tenant will cost you a month's rent.

I also encourage you to read *How to Rent Vacation Properties by Owner* (Second Edition) by Christine Hrib-Karpinski. She's developed an excellent approach to handling the ins and outs of renting your second home, wherever you may live.

If you decide to manage a rental property yourself, provide the tenant with a post office box address to which to send the rent, and a phone number to call in an emergency. Find a local handyman or maintenance company to check the property periodically and respond in an emergency. The tenant should have their phone number as well. Be sure you set a ceiling for costs, above which all repairs or maintenance must be approved by you in advance.

12

Negotiate Your Way to Wealth

People search endlessly for good deals in real estate, like panning for gold flakes in river gravel. However, you are much less likely to find a good deal than put one together yourself.

Deals that you put together yourself may bear the stamp of your personality. That is why I use the term *creative deals* to describe deals a bit out of the ordinary, due to some elements contributed by one or more of the participants. The thing that makes a deal creative may be quite small, but it's enough to make the transaction attractive.

Such deals almost always have to produce win/win situations, or at the least have the appearance of doing so. You will find a lot of additional information in *Creating Good Deals*, one of my CDs in the series, *Partnering for Profits*.

There are two approaches in putting together a creative deal, both of which can be combined for a single deal. One approach is structuring the deal, and the other is negotiating. Newcomers, of course, are going to find themselves up against people who have experience and skills in both of these approaches.

On the other hand, those experienced at the game rarely expect newcomers to be creative. If the element being introduced is truly win/win, they will welcome it.

Structuring a deal involves selecting the elements that go into it, such as the type of financing to be used. *Negotiating* a deal usually consists of persuading the other parties that the deal's conditions are in their interest as well as yours, or that they will receive something of value in return for what they concede to you. You can structure a deal on your own, but you normally have to negotiate it with other people.

Structuring a Deal

You are required to do so many time-consuming things before actually purchasing a property that you might start feeling like a student trying to pass an exam. The examiner throws all kinds of impossible questions at you, and you desperately strive to find passable answers. However, that's not what is really happening. You need to step back from it all and, in a calm and unhurried moment, look at what you are actually doing.

What *are* you doing? You are making two separate but interconnected deals, the first with the seller of the property, and the second with the lender to provide a mortgage on the property. You are not Donald Trump, but neither (in all likelihood) is the seller. The lender is not a cog in the machine of world capitalism; he or she would like to do this deal as much as the seller and you, because without a deal there is no commission. Never lose sight of the fact that you are dealing with two people—the seller and lender—with their own agendas and their own likes and dislikes.

The real estate agent may be representing you or the seller, but he or she wants a deal to be completed also—for the commission. That makes at least four people, including you, who want a deal to go through.

Handling Last-Minute Requests
As the buyer, you are not the only one interested in the deal's structure. Sellers often want late changes in a deal. For example, the

seller may not want to vacate the property for some time after the sale. Sellers often don't make such requests until the deal approaches closing, or even until closing day.

The seller's last-minute request might strike you as an unreasonable demand, or even a potential deal breaker. But think it through. A more rewarding approach may be to treat it simply as a requested change in deal structure for which the seller should be willing to give something in exchange. Does the seller have something in mind as an exchange item?

Instead of jumping in immediately with your own counter-demand, it can often work to your advantage to allow the opposite party to suggest something to exchange. You may be surprised by a seller's generosity and sometimes receive more than you would have thought of asking for, or be offered something that would almost certainly have been refused if you had asked for it.

Avoiding Confrontation

Think of a deal as the sum of its parts. The most important part to you, the buyer, is most likely the financing. It's usually something entirely different to the seller. Sellers may wonder how they can give you less, and naturally, you wonder how they can give you more. That's when fireworks can erupt.

Most people who stay in this business long enough will hear about deals that morphed into adversarial situations. After all, the traditional approach to negotiations has focused on intimidating your "opponent." But preventing an adversarial situation from developing is a much better strategy.

For instance, you've no doubt heard that you can outwit the other party by sitting with your back to the window so that the light shines in your opponent's face. Or that you should arrive first and sit far away from the door, so that your opponent has to cross the room to come to you. Or spread your papers over all the available desk space, claiming it as yours. Such ploys are ridiculous and only set the stage for hostility.

The better approach is to rid your thought process of emotions. Don't think of negotiating as "us against them"; rather, think of yourself as negotiating on behalf of someone else. Think of yourself as an intermediary for the buyer to whom you will be held accountable. This mind game works much more effectively in practice than you might think.

As the intermediary, other parties will influence you less if you think in "third-party" terms. Your thought processes will be clearer and your involvement in the deal will be less volatile.

Negotiating with Sellers
You are much more likely to have negotiations with sellers than lenders. Regardless, humans like symmetry—the idea that there's balance in compromise. You give me this, and I give you that, in equal measure.

When there's the perception of apparent symmetry, you are much more likely to get what you ask for. For example, if a seller wants to insert a clause in the contract that you will not chop down a favorite tree unless necessary, in exchange he or she may offer to include expensive gardening equipment with the property.

Try to be as accommodating as possible with sellers' requests, as long as you get something in return. However, don't accept any condition that might affect the resale value of the property, such as promising that the building or land must always, or never be, used for certain purposes. Many of these demands cannot be enforced legally anyway. If the property were found to be sitting on a vast oil reservoir, I'd want the option of building an oil well in the backyard! The same holds for gold mines.

Your due diligence investigation can lead to a renegotiated price too. For example, a property inspection that cost you $450 turns up termite damage that can only be seen from inside the crawlspace. You change the purchase price by offering $2,000 less to cover your inspection cost, the termite treatment and to hold the seller harmless for future infestations. Now, rather than start the whole process over again with someone else, the seller accepts your lower bid.

To some extent, every negotiation is a poker game. Who's bluffing? Who will fold? Who will walk away if they don't get what they ask for? If someone knows that you almost certainly will not walk away no matter what, you will probably not get what you demand.

It's Not Always about Money

No property is going to be perfect. When you look closely, you can always find fault. If your outlook is essentially negative, or you lack the commitment to act, you will always find sufficient reasons not to complete a deal. If you intend to act and have a generally positive attitude, you can usually extract concessions from the seller that more than make up for any shortcomings in the property.

I have bought properties that I might otherwise have walked away from because I wanted to establish an ongoing business relationship with the lender or agent involved in the deal. This is how an investor thinks differently from a one-time purchaser. The investor may see more potential value in the relationship with the lender, or agent, than in the actual property. I try not to waste my time, or that of other people, so I never walk unless pushed. On the other hand, I never sit still for lies, dishonesty or anything that I think might be illegal.

If you believe that negotiations are likely, make out a wish list of things that you would want as concessions. Classify them as small, medium and large. Then put them in the back of your mind where no one can discover them. You may never need them, but they may add to your confidence just by being held in reserve. All you are seeking is a deal that's fair for everybody and only slightly in your favor. It's hard to be more reasonable than that.

Need a Lawyer?

Do you need a lawyer to represent you? You may, if the seller has one and presents a boilerplate agreement for you to sign. However, if you understand all the clauses in the proposed agreement, introducing a lawyer into the negotiations may cause the seller to bring one too, and believe me, that may not help. If you do have a lawyer, he or she is there only to protect you from making a mistake.

Never rely on a lawyer to make a decision for you on whether to buy or sell. This is because lawyers are trained to look for things that can go wrong, not things that are likely to work out. A good lawyer should have a negative outlook, and a good investor shouldn't.

Negotiating with Lenders

Lenders are tough to negotiate with, not necessarily because they are tough individuals, but because they don't have much wiggle room.

They have already made up their minds about you as a credit risk. All you can really negotiate with a lender are the conditions of a loan. Most lenders have formulas in place for this. For most things that lenders concede, they charge higher rates of interest. The concessions may or may not be worth it. But sometimes, they'll surprise you with a small concession. That's good! It means that the lender sees potential in you as a real estate investor and would like to do business with you again.

13

Show Me the Money: Various Ways to Realize a Profit

Your real estate investments will be shaped, to a great extent, by the kind of financing you obtain. Therefore, your earliest strategic thinking should be about your appearance of creditworthiness. Once you buy a property with an ARM, for example, the clock has started ticking and you need to have plans to sell it or refinance it in a timely way.

To succeed as a real estate investor, however, you must have plans and strategies to achieve your goals. As goals, most of us want wealth, health and happiness. Such goals are vague, as are most people's strategies for achieving them.

However, those goals need not be vague, not if you define them in terms of real estate. In other words, what property holdings would it take for you to enjoy wealth, health and happiness? Owning a home and beach house would be more than enough for some. Others might need a mansion in town, a bunch of rental properties, and a retreat in the mountains. But what these people share is a goal expressed in terms of property. That focuses them on becoming successful real estate investors according to their own ambitions.

How about You?

How many, and what kind, of properties do you want to own? Until we own at least one property, most of us have no idea. If you had told me ten years ago what I would own today, I would have laughed in disbelief. But it's not so much about how many properties you gather, as it is about the fact that you have something real and achievable as a goal.

Your age, family status and present financial resources will help define your goal. They should not be seen as obstacles, but as realities of life that suggest appropriate courses of action.

Set a goal for yourself by selecting some kind of property in a price range you will qualify for, in a suitable area. That goal may change. It may grow bigger or smaller. But now, at least you have a goal.

You can also determine what kind of strategies might suit you best. Here are a few of the better known:

- **Buy/Hold/Occupy.** The primary objectives here are buying a house or other property, using it as your primary residence, building equity by paying off the mortgage, and benefiting from the property's appreciation in value as the years pass.

- **Buy/Hold/Rent/Cash Flow**. This calls for buying a property and holding it as a rental property. The property generates cash flow through rents. As the owner pays down the mortgage, equity grows. The owner benefits from the property's appreciating value.

- **Buy/Rehab/Sell for Profit.** In this strategy, the emphasis is on unlocking a fixer-upper's hidden value through rehab. It can be both a short- and long-term approach. By buying the property at below-market price due to its condition, and restoring the property to neighborhood standards, the owner realizes faster that normal appreciation of the home's value and can cash in on the "built-in" equity of the property.

- **Flip.** Flipping is a quick in, quick out strategy. It requires the purchase of fixers or distressed properties, rehabbing them rapidly, and selling them without delay. The owner has no intention of residing in the property, nor of renting it. Finding a sufficient inventory of flippable homes can be a serious obstacle to realizing long-term success.

What Kind of Property Should You Initially Buy?

I've already mentioned that for many, a home should be their first purchase. If you are paying rent, a house almost always should be your first real estate acquisition. The kind of property—single family, condo, townhouse, duplex or multi-unit apartment building—is not as important as the fact that you own property. You are in the game. You are no longer on the outside looking in.

How Long Should You Wait before Selling?

If you have used an ARM to buy a property, it is usually a good idea to sell before the adjustable rate kicks in. It is also usually a good idea not to wait until the last minute before doing so. Being a year early is better than being a month late.

If the house or condo is a fixer-upper, don't sell before you've rehabbed the property. Most real estate investors are usually willing to part with any property if the price is right. However, I never depend on making a quick sale. The only time you can lose money in real estate is by selling. If you can't get the price you want, hold onto the property until you do.

For planning over extended periods, it is realistic to assume that properties will appreciate in value by 5 percent each year, thanks to *compound interest*. Compound interest is interest which is then added onto the original amount of money that generates it. Thus, if the value of a $100,000 house increases 5 percent a year, or $5,000, its value increases to $105,000 in year two. The house then generates another 5 percent interest, which amounts to $5,250. So at the end of year two, the house is now valued at $110,250.

One last tip: Never refuse a good offer because you have
attached a long-term label to a property. Sell it and buy two others.

What Type of Investor Do You Want to Be?
"He who plants a garden, plants happiness."

—Chinese Proverb

There are four basic types of real estate investor: (1) safe/secure;
(2) moderate; (3) risk taker; and (4) full-time real estate investment
freak. Let's see which one fits you best.

Safe/secure investors own their homes. Little by little, month
by month, they made that first-of-the-month mortgage payment
and now they sit atop a very nice nest egg. They don't rule out altogether the idea of investing in properties, but they are extremely
uncomfortable about using their house to collateralize another mortgage. To them, the risks will usually outweigh the benefits, and they
won't get into the game unless an opportunity is a virtual slam-dunk.
Besides, they've got their retirements to think about.

Moderate investors often own one or two additional properties
as well as their homes. They like to take small, educated steps. To
them, their investments seem lackluster. The grass is always greener
in other people's deals. But then again, they hold very safe properties in very mature, stable areas. Not much growth in value year after
year and rents are pretty staid too. But if they decide to sell, they
know they'll at least get back what they put into the property.

Risk takers put possibilities ahead of potential drawbacks. For
them, money is the means to something better, rather than the goal
itself. On balance, they make more deals, and more profitable ones,
than moderate investors do. They look at every deal from every angle
and can discern the hidden value in some properties, and the hidden
dangers in others.

Full-time real estate investment freaks eat, sleep and drink real estate. When they are not structuring deals for themselves, they are doing so for friends. Unlike some people, who never see opportunities, freaks see so many that they have to avoid tripping over them. Investment freaks tend to have a solid foundation in real estate and take action quickly. Their outlook is that they have nothing to lose and everything to gain.

It is easy to see that these four niches are occupied by different personality types: cautious, content, bold, fearless. Instead of four different types of people, however, you can view them as four levels of real estate investment through which people can pass, from one to four, as they develop their skills.

I'm not saying that everyone passes through these four levels, but as *you* develop as a *Bubble Proof* real estate investor, these are the levels through which you are likely to pass.

At which of these four levels do you see yourself as an investor today? The answer to that may depend on your risk tolerance. If you are risk averse, you're likely at the first level. If you can tolerate limited risk but not more, you're likely on the second level. If you have a more devil-may-care personality, you may start out on the third level.

Not that there's anything wrong with being cautious! As with any kind of investing, caution pays off in real estate, especially for beginners who have yet to learn the rules of the game. However, some experienced investors are held back by their extreme caution, and always will be. These are the real type one investors. Lifelong type two investors often lack the drive that motivates others to become type three risk takers as they gain confidence.

How do you end up as a type four, full-time investor? Well, one success leads to another. You learn to make quick decisions. You know that you must change your life to change your income. Over time, you see the things you need to do to change your life, and you do them. You control your fears. With experience, you become educated in real estate. You begin to trust yourself.

Some investors neither strive for, nor really care about achieving level four status. And yet, to me they're completely successful. I've known many investors who enjoy real estate part time, almost as a hobby. They are part-time investors because they can't, or don't want to, give up a rewarding career and become a full-timer. The extra cash they make from their part-time endeavors is perfectly suitable for them.

Some investors stay with one niche aspect of real estate throughout their lives (doing fixer-uppers, say) and are perfectly happy. I've even known investors who've done real estate deals to achieve something specific, such as pay for their kids' college or buying a vacation home with cash—then walked away forever.

There are many ways to get into the game. To spread your risk or become involved in larger projects, you can invest with other people. Of course, you'll first make sure that your colleagues understand the risks of investing, and that profit is never guaranteed. But as friends and fellow investors who recognize the potential ups and downs of each transaction, you look forward to the potential that such deals hold.

My point is that you don't necessarily have to achieve "freakdom" to achieve your real estate goals…as long as you get there. You will come to better understand the relationship between cost and time. You will also gain increased understanding of the ways in which every real estate transaction has the potential for either gain or loss. You win and you lose. Yet even risk has its lighter side. Life is no fun without some risk.

Should You Worry about Diversification?

Real estate investments are not as diversifiable as stocks and bonds. You probably won't have dozens of properties to scatter around for safety's sake. All the same, investing only in beachfront condos, in a single big resort, may not be prudent, either. You're exposed to the risks of oil spills, red tides, hurricanes, or shark attacks—things not directly connected to the real estate market itself. Any one of those risks could affect all your beachfront condos.

Are you willing to accept the downside of those risks for the upside of owning highly marketable, waterfront properties? Most of us would take that chance, but only if they're located in more than one resort. That, to us, would be an effective way to diversify. But what if you only know the one area well, and not the others? The risks may be higher if you buy in another resort that you don't know as well.

The temptation is strong to repeat a success. I find it hard to resist. If you have done very well by buying a one-family rental property in a certain neighborhood and you get a chance to purchase another, I say you should grab it. Turning it down in order to buy something different elsewhere, solely for the sake of diversification, may increase rather than lower your risk. I am always interested in different kinds of properties in other areas, but never for the sake of moving eggs from one basket to another.

Tax Planning as a Profit Strategy

When you talk about investment strategies and planning for your future, you must include tax planning. Why? Because when income arrives, the tax collector is never far behind.

Effective tax planning can help you lessen, postpone, or avoid taxes in completely legal ways. Remember, there's a big difference between tax avoidance (legal) and tax evasion (illegal). Done right, tax avoidance is a strategy that can actually improve your bottom line.

Well-known deductions, such as for mortgage interest, property taxes, certain closing costs, capital gains exclusions and 1031 tax-deferred property transfers, are dear to every real estate investor's heart. Some tax rules provide for others, and although they tend to be rather complicated, your tax advisor should be able to apply them for your benefit.

Rental Tax Benefits

Three kinds of rental expenses are deductible from your federal taxes: mortgage interest, operating expense and depreciation. Since 90 percent of your early mortgage payments are actually interest payments, your resulting tax deduction can be quite large. Operating expenses such as property taxes, hazard insurance and repairs and maintenance may also be deductible. Since no land is involved in a condo purchase, the full cost of a condo can be depreciated.

These deductions can amount to a considerable annual sum. In fact, deductions are often larger than the annual rental income, thus producing negative cash flow.

With a condo, if your adjusted gross income does not exceed $100,000 and you actively participate in the management of the property, you can deduct up to $25,000 of this negative income from your other income. This should include such items as salary, dividends and interest. For adjusted gross incomes of more than $100,000, deductions are more complex.

You can carry forward losses from year to year. You can even carry all the losses forward until you sell and deduct them from the sales income. Once again, I recommend getting a real estate accountant's advice on the complexities of tax regulations. An expert accountant may suggest additional write-offs, such as deductions for advertising.

Capital Gains Tax Exclusion

As I've mentioned already, when you have owned and used a home as your principal residence for at least two of the five previous years, you can exclude a gain of up to $500,000 if you are married and filing jointly, and $250,000 if single. For instance, if a couple bought a home for $100,000 and sold it for $600,000, they would owe not a penny in federal income tax. If they sold the $100,000 house for $1 million, they would owe taxes on $400,000. (For details, *see* IRS Publication 523.)

The exclusion does **not** apply to condos. It applies to vacation homes only when they qualify as principal residences for the necessary time.

Even better, this capital gains windfall is not, as many people think, a once-in-a-lifetime offer. You can make use of it every two years. If you sell in less than two years, because of a change in your place of employment, health or unforeseen circumstances, you may be able to get a reduced exclusion. Examples of unforeseen circumstances include divorce, legal separation, job loss, and the birth of twins or triplets. If unforeseen circumstances cause you to sell after one year instead of two, you typically receive half the exclusion.

14

Equip Yourself with a Millionaire Mindset

Becoming a millionaire is largely a matter of mental attitude. If you are determined to become one, you will. In the following examples, I prepare you for this transformation by contrasting the attitudes of "millionaires" with "average people."

This is not to say that *all* millionaires have the right attitude, and *all* average people don't. I am simply using millionaires and average people as symbols for how active, prosperous people think. I realize that many millionaires consider themselves to be average people. However, I assure you—even the attitudes of the most down-home millionaires are different from those of the people they blend in with.

Again, it's differences in attitude, not makes of cars or brands of shoes. Nor is this about social snobbery. Some millionaires get their kicks from financial performance and not their personal appearance. I heard about a gallery owner warning a new assistant *never* to judge people by how they looked. She said that half the people who bought expensive paintings looked as if they were there to remove the trash. How would the assistant know? She would wait for the customers to talk, and their attitudes would give the rich ones away.

If you want to be a millionaire, think like one. You don't need the car or the shoes, but you will need the outlook.

#1

Millionaires know what they want. Average people don't get what they want because they don't know what they want.

"Every human being is intended to have a character of his own; to be what no others are, and to do what no other can do." —William Ellery Channing

It is nice to believe in the myth that people don't know what they want because they're complicated and have all kinds of ideas swirling through their minds. People with many ideas usually know what they want. But you don't need ideas. You need character, a sense of possibilities, and a determination to act. In the real world, you get what you want, even when you think you don't know what that is. All some people want is a state of indecision and anxiety. The smart ones want real estate.

Step to Success #1

Describe the ideal property you would like to own in 12 months' time, keeping the description at an achievable economic level.

#2

Millionaires dedicate themselves to creating wealth. Average people buy lottery tickets.

You rarely see investors in casinos. That is because they get their thrills in the marketplace. They invest their gains in more property, thereby creating more wealth.

Step to Success #2

List anything you have done, in the past 12 months, which has the potential of creating wealth for you. Having a job counts.

#3

Millionaires think big. Average people try not to think big.

To learn how to do something, it is best to start small. But don't hide from challenges. A big Wall Street investor once told me that he had invested a second time in a project with someone whose first project failed. Why? He believed in his partner. Think big. People are looking for someone like you.

Step to Success #3

Describe your ideal real estate investment, if you had a million dollars. What would you invest in if you and fellow investors had ten million?

#4

Millionaires see opportunities in life. Average people see obstacles.

This is the land of opportunity. Unfortunately, opportunities are rarely presented to us readymade and shining. Many people have more or less a prospector's viewpoint of opportunity—they expect to see precious metal shining in dull gravel. Millionaires know that they have to make opportunities happen, not wait for them.

Step to Success #4

Describe honestly three opportunities you missed out on in the past 12 months. Is any single cause responsible for more than one of them? Work on that cause. Also, right now, is there an opportunity in front of your nose that you have yet to see?

#5

Millionaires cause things to happen. Average people have things happen to them.

When you take control of your life, random events may still catch you by surprise, but they never assume control over it. Once you are responsible for the happenings in your life, you have a much better chance of liking what takes place. If you don't cause changes, other people and things will.

Step to Success #5

If you feel someone is more responsible than you for something that has happened in your life, good or bad, retell the story with you taking full responsibility for what occurred.

#6

Millionaires play to win. Average people try not to lose.

In my real estate business, as in my life, I personally try to find as many win/win situations as I can, and I go out of my way to avoid bruising one-on-one competitions with others. I prefer to expend my energy on other things, but when I get involved in something, I go all out to win. That does not mean that someone else has to lose. My definition of winning is achieving what I set out to do, not showing myself to be better at something than someone else. What are your chances of winning if you only try not to lose? Let me tell you that they are not very good.

Step to Success #6

Using a realistic scenario, describe how, in the next 12 months, you will be able to buy a really desirable piece of real estate.

#7

Millionaires are leaders because they promote their values and beliefs. Average people know that no one cares about their values, and they don't want to appear pushy.

At a party, a friend joined a group of people who were standing off to one side. The people were all polite, considerate and boring. Then they were joined by another guest, a textiles millionaire. He proceeded to discuss a variety of topics with them, and was so entertaining that soon, half the party gathered 'round to listen and laugh. He naturally brought people into his sphere of influence, just by sharing his thoughts. Before his arrival, the little group had bored one another. They probably all had interesting things to say, but chose not to communicate them. No one would be inspired to invest with them or follow their lead.

Step to Success #7

Take three minutes to talk about yourself with people who will become intrigued by what you stand for. Use the time well.

#8

Millionaires are bigger than their problems. Average people are smaller.

A large number of entertainers first got into performing publicly while overcoming a handicap, such as a stammer or overwhelming shyness. In much the same way, people become millionaires by overcoming their problems.

Step to Success #8

Write down your three biggest problems, and then something that would alleviate each problem. If any solution helps with more than one problem, concentrate on it. If nothing helps, are you going places or will you stay home with your problems?

#9

Millionaires admire ability in others. Average people resent it.

Many times, millionaires choose to expand their holdings by extending partnerships to people whose ability they admire. For example, in setting up limited liability partnerships to buy properties, they might offer investing partnerships to fellow millionaires, and offer a "sweat equity" partnership to an entrepreneur with no capital, but who has an uncanny knack for finding opportunities through hard work.

Step to Success #9

Describe how someone you know handled an everyday incident in a truly admirable way.

#10

Millionaires take chances to gain profit. Average people are afraid to jeopardize their weekly paycheck.

Although people who depend on results to be rewarded are at a much higher risk than regular wage earners, their future work possibilities are greater and have fewer boundaries. In this way, their risk for reward over the long term may be less. Wage earners become categorized more easily and are in greater danger of being replaced by automation or overseas workers.

Step to Success #10

If you must have a regular paycheck, you'll have to become a millionaire in your free time. Make the time, make the plans, get the financing, do what you have to do.

#11

Millionaires never say, "This is enough, I don't want more." Average people are grateful for what they have and know their place.

There is a saying that you gain peace of mind by accepting what you have. That may depend on what you have and what you want to have. Millionaires generally want to have more than they presently possess, and it doesn't seem to interfere much with their peace of mind.

Step to Success #11

If you know what you want, you know what you have to do to get it. How far along are you? If you haven't started, write down the date you will start. That should be today.

#12

Millionaires use business plans to control their present financial resources and accumulate more. Average people have no plans to accumulate financial resources.

One wealthy investor buys condos in up-and-coming neighborhoods, waits for the neighborhoods to peak in popularity, sells the condos at the peak, and uses the proceeds to buy more condos at lower prices in other up-and-coming neighborhoods. This is all he does. It is part of his plan. He is more interested in steady growth and no surprises than startling profits, though he has those too.

Step to Success #12

If you lack the financial resources, credit, and income to get started, put together a business plan. State your 12-month, 3-year and 5-year goals.

Putting It All Together

"Courage is the mastery of fear—not absence of it."

—Mark Twain

I'm happy to have inspired many people, in motivational talks and meetings of my groups, to do something about their lives. One danger of a nondemanding society is that you can drift along for years, just getting by, without ever facing up to the meaning of your life. I call this a danger because after a certain point, you can find yourself trapped in inertia, unable to find fulfillment when you feel a deep spiritual need to do so.

Using your abilities and talents for the betterment of yourself and others gives meaning to life. The more power and prosperity you gather, the more you can help others, if you so choose. Wealth provides options. How you use your wealth is how others will judge you. If you choose not to act, and use your talents and abilities to help yourself and others, they may judge you for that too.

America is the land of opportunity. In the past, opportunity has been limited to those with wealth, connections, or extraordinary luck, foresight or courage. Today you are in the right place at the right time. All you have to do is open your eyes, understand what you see and act accordingly.

I think I can fairly claim that I have spelled it out for you. It is now up to you, if you care enough, to do something about it. Consider what you have to lose, which is probably very little. Also consider what you have to gain, which is almost certainly a great deal. What is holding you back?

This book is a call to action. This book alerts you to a great opportunity in America today to buy property and become one of the owners of this land. It is impossible to say, at the time of writing, how long this opportunity will last. Obviously a rise in mortgage interest rates will have a chilling effect on the real estate market. If such a rise in interest rates is high, it will cut off many people's options to buy. In other words, there is an urgency to act now while you still can.

There will be other opportunities in other fields, no doubt. The thing that makes this opportunity unique, however, is that almost anyone can qualify. The main hindrance to participation is you yourself. You must know what you want. You must be determined to get it. You must act!

Those three requirements are necessary for almost everything of value, including close personal relationships. People who love life and know how to value it deserve its treasures. One of those treasures is financial security for you and your loved ones. Right now the gate is open to property owning and real estate investment. Walk through it.

Some Terms Used in Real Estate

Adjustable-rate mortgage (ARM): A mortgage that consists of two terms, the first of which has a fixed rate of interest, and the second an adjustable rate.

Adjustment: State and local taxes are often negotiated between buyers and sellers. The resulting agreement is called an adjustment.

Affidavit: A sworn statement that you sign regarding various claims you have made, such as your employment status and bank account information.

Agent service bureau: A real estate agency whose agents pay fees rather than percentages of their commissions, and thus favor higher price properties to cover their costs. RE/MAX is the biggest franchise.

All Inclusive Trust Deed (AITD): A deed that secures a wrap-around loan that incorporates an existing loan with a new loan made by the property seller.

Amortization: The gradual increases of your equity in a property as you pay off your mortgage. Fully amortizing payments pay off the principal within the term of the mortgage.

Annual percentage rate (APR): The rate of interest for a loan per year, which may or may not include other costs or fees.

Appraisal: An estimate of the value of a property by a professional expert.

Appreciation: Increase in property value.

ARM: *See* Adjustable-rate mortgage.

Assign: To transfer your property rights, or contract rights, to another.

Assumption fee: The fee paid to the lender when the buyer takes over the payments on a loan previously made to the seller. The buyer usually pays this fee.

Balloon mortgage: A mortgage that has monthly payments on a thirty-year amortization schedule, until it comes to the end of its five- or seven-year term, when the entire loan balance must be paid off.

Brokerage company: Independent real estate agents in your community are likely to be associated with a traditional brokerage company that restricts its activities to brokerage, leaving the agents free to refer you to lenders and service providers of their own choosing.

Building inspection: Examination of a building by an independent authorized home inspector.

Buyer's agent: A real estate agent who works for the buyer rather than the seller. A buyer's agent represents you exclusively, and you are bound contractually to that agent.

Cap: A limit placed on adjustments to the interest rate or payment level as protection for borrowers.

Casualty insurance: Insurance that covers property damage from fire, weather and most other causes.

Closing: The closing or settlement is the last step in purchasing a property. At the end of a successful closing, the property is yours.

Closing date: The sales contract generally has an estimated closing or commitment date. After your loan application is accepted and you have signed the commitment letter, a closing date will be fixed.

Closing costs: Costs at closing usually range from 2 to 7 percent of the loan amount.

Commitment letter: This document gives the mortgage amount, term of the loan, loan origination fee, discount points, annual percentage rate and monthly payments, as well as stating the date by which you must accept and formally apply for the loan.

Contingency: A condition that must be fulfilled before a contract can be regarded as legally binding.

Credit bureau: One of three nationwide private agencies that produce credit reports and credit scores on private consumers. The three bureaus are TransUnion, Equifax, and Experian.

Credit report: A summary by a credit bureau of your credit transactions and a record of outstanding debts, foreclosure or bankruptcy.

Credit score: Your credit standing in digitized form. The credit scoring system is known as the FICO score, for the Fair Isaac Company that developed it. Three nationwide credit bureaus assign scores: TransUnion, Equifax, and Experian.

Deed: Document transferring ownership of a property.

Depreciation: Loss in value of an asset over its estimated useful life.

Down payment: Amount of payment in cash by the purchaser. Traditionally the down payment on a building was 20 percent of the total price. Mortgages available today permit you to pay as little as 3 to 5 percent of the purchase price.

Due diligence: Process of, before finalizing a purchase, making your own efforts to ensure that all is well with the property.

Earnest money: Cash deposit to show good faith, or serious intent, on the part of the purchaser. The earnest money is deposited into an escrow account.

Employer-Assisted Housing (EAH): EAH loans are often used toward down payments, closing costs, and interest rate buy downs, which can lower monthly mortgage payments.

Equifax: *See* Credit bureau.

Equity: The percentage of ownership in a property fully paid for by a person.

Experian: *See* Credit bureau.

Fannie Mae: Nickname for a federally chartered private company that purchases mortgages from lenders and sells mortgage-backed securities on the capital markets. *See also* Freddie Mac. These two government-backed companies each have a series of mortgages that they issue though approved lenders.

Federal Truth in Lending Act: Congressional act that requires lenders to inform you about the terms and costs of a loan at the time you are given an application.

Final walk-through inspection: A last-minute walk-through inspection of the property before closing, often specified by a clause in the sales contract.

Fixed-rate mortgage: A mortgage in which the interest rate cannot be changed or adjusted.

Fixer-Upper: A house with more apparent than real damage, which can be put on the market again after some renovation.

Flip: Purchase and immediate resale of property.

Freddie Mac: Nickname for a federally chartered private company that purchases mortgages from lenders and sells mortgage-backed securities on the capital markets. *See also* Fannie Mae. These two government-backed companies each have a series of mortgages that they issue though approved lenders.

Gentrification: Socioeconomic rise of a neighborhood.

Graduated payment mortgage (GPM): A fixed-rate mortgage in which negative amortization reduces early payments at the cost of raising later payments.

Home Equity Line of Credit: Using a credit line to borrow against the equity in your home has become a popular source of consumer credit.

Interest rate: Percentage of loan paid per year by the borrower to the lender in addition to the principal.

Interest-only payments: Mortgage payments that cover only the interest due, without any amortization.

Jumbo mortgages: Mortgages for larger amounts than Fannie Mae or Freddie Mac mortgages and generally with an interest rate that is 0.25 or 0.5 percent higher. Instead of being backed by the government, they are bought and pooled by large financial companies.

Lease option: A deal to buy a house within a certain time by making a down payment and paying rent, with a fixed amount of the monthly rent being put toward the purchase price. If the purchase is not made as agreed, the down payment is forfeited.

Leverage: Use of borrowed funds to increase purchasing power and, ideally, to increase the profitability of an investment.

Liability insurance: Insurance that covers injury to visitors of a building.

Lien: A charge against income or a property making it security for the payment of debt.

Loan continuing costs: Some lenders require you to pay continuing costs throughout the term of the loan, in addition to closing costs.

Loan discount points: Lenders charge fees called discount points to lower the interest rate of a mortgage. For a 30-year mortgage, one discount point—1 percent of loan total—generally lowers the interest rate by 0.125 percent.

Loan origination fee: This fee covers processing costs and is often quoted in points, that is, as a percentage of the total loan.

Market value: The highest price a buyer, willing but not compelled to buy, would pay, and the lowest price a seller, willing but not compelled to sell, would accept.

Mortgage: A loan you take out on a property that you repay over a specified time.

Mortgage insurance: Mortgage insurance paid by people who are considered high risk.

Negative amortization: A process in which none of the principal, and not all the interest, is paid back in mortgage payments, and each month the shortfall in interest payment is added to the principal. This amounts to the lender extending an additional loan each month to the borrower.

No/low down payment mortgages: Mortgages that require from as little as 3 percent to no down payment on purchase. Some of these mortgages come with few or no income requirements for those with very good credit.

Note: A document that acknowledges a debt and promises payment.

Occupancy date: Date on which you will take possession of the property after it has been bought.

Offer: Document consisting of price you want to pay, survey and legal description of the property you expect to receive, down payment amount, mortgage amount with interest rate, earnest money amount, closing date, occupancy date, furniture, fixtures, or other items to be included with the property; and contingencies, which may include financing, repairs, home inspections, appraisal, environmental concerns, clear title, offer expiration date, and type of financing you are seeking.

Operating expenses: Amount paid to maintain a property, such as property taxes, utilities and hazard insurance.

Partnership: An agreement between two or more entities to invest or go into business together.

Passive income: Income generated from rents, royalties, dividends, interest and gains from sales of securities.

Pick a pay loan: This type of loan gives borrowers a choice of payment amounts with minimum payments that may be only half the amount of customary payments.

Principal: The amount of money loaned without counting interest, costs, or fees.

Promissory note: Borrower's note to the lender detailing the terms of the mortgage and how the borrower will pay it.

Property search: In a traditional property search, a real estate agent drove you from house to house until you found one that was right for you. Online listings have taken much of the driving and legwork out of this process.

Rate of return: Percentage relationship between the earnings and cost of an investment.

Real estate agent: A professional who acts as a liaison between the buyer and seller of a property, and who usually represents, and is paid by, the seller. *See* Buyer's agent.

Real estate services companies: If you want a lot of professional advice and services in a one-stop shopping arrangement, an agent who works with a real estate services company may have more to offer you. The majority of these companies belong to a national franchise, such as Century 21. Their agents have the freedom to make independent referrals, just like agents who work with traditional brokerage companies do.

Refinance: To replace an old loan with a new loan.

Seller financing: Financing assumed by the seller as part of the purchase of the property.

Settlement: *See* Closing.

Settlement statement: A document declaring which closing costs the buyer and seller each will pay.

Survey: A map or plot plan depicting the property boundaries, improvements, easements, rights of way, encroachments, and other physical features.

Tax lien: A debt attached to a property for failure to pay taxes.

Termite inspection: The seller usually pays for a termite inspection, which is required in many areas before a property can be sold. The inspection certificate should state that the building is free of termite infestation and termite damage.

Title: Document showing evidence of ownership.

Title insurance: You, the buyer, usually pay to take out an insurance policy for the lender against the possibility that the property title may not be clear. For a small additional sum, the lender's policy can be extended to cover you. The policy remains in effect as long as you own the property, even after the mortgage has been paid off or refinanced.

Title search: A search required by most lenders to make sure the title to the property is clear of encumbrances. Encumbrances can include IRS liens and claims against the property for unpaid bills. The seller must settle all such encumbrances before, or at, the closing.

Trading up and down: People trade up when their houses have gotten too small and trade down when their houses have gotten too large.

TransUnion: *See* Credit bureau.

Vacancy rate: The percentage of units unoccupied or not rented.

Wraparound mortgage: A mortgage that includes an underlying mortgage in its balance.